# ECONOMICS
# AND
# POLICYMAKING

Recent Titles in
Contributions in Economics and Economic History
*Series Editor: Robert Sobel*

# ECONOMICS AND POLICYMAKING
## The Tragic Illusion

# EUGENE J. MEEHAN

Contributions in Economics and
Economic History, Number 47

**Greenwood Press**
Westport, Connecticut
London, England

**Library of Congress Cataloging in Publication Data**

Meehan, Eugene J.
  Economics and policymaking.

  (Contributions in economics and economic history,
ISSN 0084-9235; no. 47)
  Bibliography: p.
  Includes index.
  1. Economic policy.   2. Economics.   I. Title.
II. Series.
HD87.M43            338.9'001            81-20331
ISBN 0-313-23313-6 (lib. bdg.)            AACR2

Library of Congress Cataloging Card Number: 81-20331
ISBN: 0-313-23313-6
ISSN: 0084-9235

First published in 1982

Greenwood Press
A division of Congressional Information Service, Inc.
88 Post Road West
Westport, Connecticut 06881

Printed in the United States of America

10 9 8 7 6 5 4 3 2 1

# Contents

# Acknowledgments

Much of the preliminary work for this study was completed while I was a Fellow in the Center for Metropolitan Studies at the University of Missouri-St. Louis. A fellowship at the Netherlands Institute for Advanced Study in 1980-81 provided a perfect environment for completing the research and preparing the manuscript. I am most grateful to both organizations.

# ECONOMICS
# AND
# POLICYMAKING

_____ 1 _____ Introduction

My primary purpose in this volume is to answer two closely related questions about economics as it is currently taught and practiced in the United States. First, are the products of economics adequate to enable a competent policymaker, public or private, to create policies that are defensible, reliable, and corrigible out of experience? Can economics produce the kinds of knowledge that policymakers must have to perform effectively? Second, how can the performance of economics with respect to policymaking be improved? What are the criteria of adequacy that should be applied to economic inquiries, and to the knowledge claims they generate, when the purpose is to contribute to reasoned and defensible policymaking?

The human significance of the two questions requires little argument; the consequentiality of the economic dimension of individual and social life is not disputed. Indeed, if the basic economic problems facing human society cannot be resolved, development of human capacity in other areas is unlikely to occur, and in the extreme case, survival becomes problematic. In the United States, and most of the rest of the Western world at least, efforts to cope with economic affairs are directed (or perhaps rationalized) using the basic intellectual apparatus that has evolved within economics. Such "applications" of economic knowledge have a vital impact on the lives of countless millions of persons. It follows that the quality of the available body of economic knowledge, its usefulness and reliability for directing real world affairs is a matter of concern for nearly everyone.

The examination of contemporary American economics is carried out within the broadest and most general framework possible—principally in epistemological-methodological terms. The focus of criticism is the overall conceptual-theoretical framework that most economists share—the basic "paradigm" in economics, to use Thomas Kuhn's illuminating construct[1]—and the various approaches to inquiry that have developed around that base. For the most part, the validity of data and the accuracy of logical calculation are not questioned. Criticism concentrates instead on the goals that economists pursue, the instruments created within economics to achieve those goals, and the relation between the purposes and products of economics and the needs and purposes of the competent policymaker. The framework needed for examining those complex relations is supplied by a theory of knowledge or epistemology.

There are a number of compelling reasons for approaching the relations between economics and policymaking at the level of the underlying paradigm. First, and most important, that is the point where the major weaknesses in the discipline are found and therefore the level where corrections will have to be made before economics can become a useful and reliable guide to reasoned human action. At the present time, very few of the products of economics can be used by policymakers seeking a defensible basis for action. The principal source of that inadequacy is found in the set of fundamental assumptions that guide economic inquiry; the primary evidence of inadequacy appears in the knowledge that has actually been created or produced. Economics does not at present create the tools that competent policymakers must have for developing defensible policies. Moreover, so long as the current paradigm, and its associated modes of inquiry, is maintained, that situation will continue. And since the reward system within economics, as in other academic disciplines, strongly supports maintenance of the status quo, fundamental change is unlikely, particularly in the short run.

A second reason for concentrating on the underlying structure of assumptions in economics rather than the particulars of individual studies is the extreme disparity of the work carried out in the discipline. At present, economics comprises a congeries of fields and subfields directed at a wide range of phenomena. If performance with respect to policymaking is to improve substantially, criticism must reach nearly all of these subfields effectively. Obviously, criticism aimed at one specific type of inquiry, or at one limited field of study, is unlikely to influence those concerned with other phenomena or using other methods and techniques. To be effective, the criticism must be generalized. Focusing on the overall conceptual-theoretical framework, and related methods of inquiry, provides a way of reaching nearly all of economics through a single channel. Epistemological-methodological criticism is both broad enough to reach most of the subfields and precise enough to be applied and tested within each one of them. Finally, such criticism is not merely negative and destructive. Because it identifies the reasons for inadequacy, it offers a point of departure for efforts at improvement. And because the critical structure links performance to purpose, it provides a way of identifying improvements where they occur.

The third reason for choosing a generalized focus for the critical effort is the extent to which the economic paradigm has been incorporated into the fabric of American political and intellectual life. Economics has been accorded very high intellectual status, particularly in the recent past; its influence has become institutionalized to a truly remarkable degree. The primary vehicle for that influence has been the economic paradigm, the overall conception of what economics is about and how economic inquiries should be pursued. The influence of the paradigm extends far beyond its obvious importance to such agencies as the President's Council of Economic Advisors, the Federal Reserve Board, the Office of Management and Budget, the various committees in Congress concerned with economic affairs, and even to private business. The influence that economics exerts on intellectual life through the public schools and the various media is probably even greater than its influence on public and private organizations. And within the academic community, proselytizing on behalf of an "economics approach" to inquiry, particularly in social science, has been widespread since World War II.[2] In economic affairs, most Americans have marched to the beat of a single drum for nearly half a century. The same situation is found in most other Western nations, notably Great Britain, West Germany, the Netherlands, and Scandinavia. If, as will be argued below, economics has been grossly oversold in the past, criticism at any other level would be an ineffective remedy for the harm that has already been done.

The extent of the economics "oversell" and its implications for future improvement bears additional emphasis. In government, private business, schools, media, and even specialized economic organizations such as labor unions, research centers, or producer associations, the basic economic paradigm is accepted without serious questioning—or even awareness. Not surprisingly, economists share the generally favorable appraisal of disciplinary capacity, though some might dissent from the astonishing optimism of Nobel laureate Paul A. Samuelson, writing at the end of the 1950s: "many economists feel technologically unemployed: having helped to banish the worst economic diseases of capitalism, they feel like the ear surgeons whose function modern antibiotics has reduced to a low level of priority."[3] The effect of more than two decades of economics teaching in an atmosphere of such sanguinity and self-confidence has not, to my knowledge, been examined systematically. But if Kuhn's conception of "normal science" is even approximately correct,[4] the profession is by now virtually impervious to external criticism and modification of the underlying paradigm will be nearly impossible—even a crisis will not suffice. Certainly that is the impression gained from extensive reading of the leading economic journals and texts.

The fact that economists themselves rarely examine their own basic assumptions, and that economic writings very seldom show any awareness of the importance of the epistemological-methodological dimensions of inquiry, provides a fourth reason for concentrating on that aspect of the discipline. Economics has been and continues to be criticized by economists, of course. Highly respected members of the profession—Joan Robinson, Robert A. Gordon, Wassily Leontief, and Kenneth Boulding, to name just a few—have pointed to serious deficiencies in disciplinary performance. In many cases, their criticisms have concentrated on the widening gap between real world experience and the substance of academic economics, but criticism directed at epistemological or methodological fundamentals is rare. As Stanley Wong noted in one of the

few published papers on economic methodology, "most methodological discussions in economics are vague and confusing debates
which are of little apparent significance to the day-to-day work
of the practicing economist."[5] Occasionally, a prominent economist will venture into the methodological arena, often under pressure of a widespread demand for relevance by the younger members
of the discipline. Thus, Wassily Leontief, in a trenchant critique
of economics published in 1971, noted *inter alia* that,

[unease among economists] . . . is caused not by the *irrelevance* of the
practical problems to which present-day economists address their efforts,
but rather by the palpable *inadequacy* of the scientific means by which they
try to solve them.[6]

Leontief's criticism would not, I think, have found widespread
support among economists, even at the time of writing. Certainly,
it had little subsequent influence on the discipline, to the extent
that can be determined from citation. Most important of all, as the
decade of the 70s ended, economics still had not produced an ex-
emplar of an alternative approach to inquiry that could serve as
guide and model for the next generation. Radical criticism coming
from a few determined and vociferous Marxists and their supporters
failed to gain significant support within the discipline, but since
they sought, in most cases, to substitute one dogma for another
rather than de-dogmatize the profession, that outcome was probably
salutory.
   The fate of the less radical critics of conventional economics,
perhaps best epitomized in the work of John Kenneth Galbraith,
was about the same, however, and that may be cause for concern
among economists and noneconomists alike. Galbraith was of
course notable for his concern with real world problems and the
role that economists might play in their solution. He spoke to the
substance of such concerns rather than to methodological and
epistemological problems. And his commitment to the basic economic paradigm remained consistent. His criticism evolved *within*
the paradigm, hence could presumably be accepted more readily
within the profession than a demand for revision of fundamentals.
But if Galbraith's influence has been substantial outside academic

economics, within the discipline that has not been the case. As a very rough indication, the *Social Sciences Citation Index* for 1979 lists more than 250 references to Galbraith's publications, but only twenty of those citations appeared in journals even remotely linked to academic economics and about half of them are found in the *Journal of Economic Issues,* which is hardly in the mainstream of the discipline. The *American Journal of Economics* contained only the three citations to Galbraith during the entire year; in the *American Economic Review* there was but one. That pattern of citations suggests that economics as a whole is not moving in the same direction as those who seek closer relations with real world concerns or everyday affairs.

The effort to bring academic economics more closely into line with practical problems went badly during the 1970s; and no serious effort was made to improve its epistemological-methodological base. Yet, unless there is a significant improvement in the basic approach to inquiry, future extensions or improvements in the knowledge produced by the discipline are likely to be impeded or inhibited completely. Even scholars in such fields as physics, which have theoretical networks so firmly established and highly elaborated that some persons can spend a lifetime wholly separated from direct observation or experiment, cannot ignore the relation between theoretical assumptions and experimental roots. Economists, who follow rather closely the pattern of inquiry in theoretical physics, have failed to take into account the essential distinction between the work carried out by an individual theorist and the knowledge content of the discipline in which the theorizing occurs. That is, if the individual theorist in physics does not need to observe directly, or even refer to experience indirectly, particularly in the short run, the *theory* being elaborated must be linked very firmly to observation and test. Confusing those two dimensions of inquiry can lead to a disastrous conception of the nature of the theoretical enterprise. Performance in use is the ultimate test of every theory in science. Economics has a long history, but the performance record is not impressive. Indeed, the absence of any well-established relation between theory and data is widely recognized and much criticized within economics. Nevertheless, there has been a discernible tendency for economics to become increasingly formal or mathematical in recent decades, thus exacerbating the problem of poor performance. The result is a serious gap in the knowledge-producing chain, a gap with especially important consequences for policymaking.

In any human endeavor, awareness of error is a prerequisite to improvement, barring serendipity. It will most often emerge from systematic efforts to deal with genuine problems. Awareness alone cannot guarantee improvement, of course, but its absence virtually ensures continued failure. Granted that human actions often are made under conditions of uncertainty that approach total ignorance, self-conscious efforts to produce expected results by known means in a specified situation at least satisfy the minimum conditions for learning. Efforts to reconstruct the assumptions on which actions depended *post hoc,* if sometimes unavoidable, are always cognitively inferior to articulation of assumptions prior to action. Retrospection greatly increases the risk of confusing what is only a rationalization after the fact with a genuine test of assumptions or theories.

To be more specific and practical, if the weakness of an underlying paradigm is unknown or ignored, efforts to improve are most likely to seek a substitution of subsystems, leaving the overall structure intact. Such efforts are doomed in advance. If a rocket trip fails because the theory of motion used in planning is mistaken, the error cannot be corrected at the level of the fuel system. A good illustration within economics appears in the reaction of economists to the deterioration of the U.S. economy during the 1970s and the apparent failure of economic policy that it signaled. By 1980, it was nearly impossible to subscribe to Samuelson's euphoric assessment of the capacity of economics to provide guidance in real world affairs. Although the need for change was widely recognized, the search for alternatives concentrated almost entirely on subsystems within economics—chiefly the substitution of monetarism for neo-Keynesian economics. The basic goals, purposes, and methods of economics remained unchanged. But the findings here suggest that a society which must choose among Marxists, monetarists, neo-Keynesians, and others who toil in economics faces a devil's choice. Like the man preparing to jump from an aircraft two miles up who is offered a choice between a silk handkerchief and a small umbrella, the chooser has little reason to suppose that the outcome will be affected very much by the choice made. An umbrella may provide a few more seconds for repentance; the ultimate outcome is identical in either case.

There is one more point to be made about epistemological-methodological criticism within economics. External criticism of the sort undertaken here may serve to locate error and misdirection and suggest remedies in very broad terms. At the moment, that seems essential. But in the long run, the improvement of economics is a matter to be carried through by economists. The outside critic may suggest criteria that should be applied to the field but the application must be made by working economists, and reflected in their work. There is no need for every economics student to become a professional epistemologist or methodologist, but competence in those areas should be built into professional training. Otherwise, those who have completed training remain dependent on external guidance and criticism, unable to produce adequate self-criticism or direct self-improvement. Training responsibility lies with economists, familiar with the substance of the discipline. It cannot be left for technicians unfamiliar with the practical problems encountered in economic field work.

The fifth and perhaps strongest reason for discussing the relations between economics and policymaking at the level of the basic paradigm is the variety of meanings that contemporary usage attaches to the term *policy.* Ordinarily, the best available evidence for the usefulness of a product is the use actually being made of it, determined by consulting the users. Unfortunately, that simple procedure cannot be followed here. And the reason lies in the diversity of meanings attached to policy and the range of instruments and actions considered acceptable forms of policy and policymaking. Claims asserting that economics has been "applied" to individual or collective affairs must be discounted heavily until the precise meaning and implications of the claim have been determined. Even in those cases where the meaning of terms has been agreed, the meaning may be inadequate and the claim will not refer to a valid test of an adequate instrument. To place intellectual activities such as policymaking on a sound intellectual footing, the meaning of fundamental terms must be specified precisely. Until that is done, the contribution that economics can make to the activity remains uncertain.

Development and deployment of an adequate conception of policy has proceeded very slowly despite substantial recent expenditures and a vast increase in academic interest. A major reason for the slow rate of conceptual improvement, in contrast to enormous technological advances in information processing, is that conceptual improvement depends on awareness of and attention to a set of analytic requirements that is usually ignored. Since those requirements are identified and justified only within a fully articulated analytic framework, they cannot be included in a simple definition of policy without explication. A policy is usually defined as a guide to action, a device for directing human actions. Historically, that meaning has simply evolved and it remains isolated from either applications or limits. Contingencies attached to the term may be impossible to determine given the meaning that tradition assigns and the way in which inquiries are managed. Reasoned criticism of policy cannot develop from such an inadequate base. Concepts such as policy must be embedded in a network of contingent relations, stated in an appropriate metalanguage, linking the concept to the purposes for which it can be used in ways that reveal both formal requirements and limits on application. Within such a framework, the meaning of *application* and *improvement* can also be stated, assuming that the framework has been generated properly. That is the approach to meaning, or definition, adopted here. It is slow, and sometimes tedious, but essential for establishing a secure foundation for future improvements.

The point of departure for reasoned criticism of any kind of human performance, whether intellectual or physical, is not an instrument whose uses can be explored forthwith but a set of purposes to be fulfilled by action and a set of limits to be observed in the pursuit of purpose. With respect to policymaking, some significant human purpose(s) must be identified and the limits within which those purposes can be satisfied must be determined. The instrument required to satisfy the purposes, in this case a policy, must lie within human competence, be amenable to test and improvement out of experience, and correspond closely enough to everyday meanings to allow the transfer of valuable prior learning into the apparatus used in systematic criticism. Further elaboration of purposes and limitations will establish fairly precisely the characteristics of the instrument required to achieve the purpose and some of the conditions governing use. The instrument then can be labeled in a way that aligns it optimally with current usage. Once that process has been carried out, the concept will have the same label or symbol, and approximately the same surface meaning, in both technical or critical language and everyday use. But the analytic context associated with the technical term provides a base for test and improvement that has no counterpart in everyday usage and may be incompatible with it.

It may appear that a relatively simple problem in definition is being complicated needlessly. But in the wider context in which the relation between economics and policymaking will be examined, the need for clarification is clear and urgent. Construed as a guide to action, a policy is a normative or evaluative instrument. For policies must focus on what should be the case, on deliberate preferences, and not what is or will be the case disregarding the element of human action. Economics, on the other hand, is certainly an empirical discipline, devoted to the study of what is the case and how events are related in certain aspects of the observable world. To ask how economics can be used in policymaking is not to ask how economists can be brought into the normative arena, or become moral philosophers. What it does raise in concrete form is the widely discussed question, What does an empirical discipline, a science, contribute to normative inquiry? Or, to invert the question, What does normative inquiry require from empirical disciplines? If the need for an empirical discipline to make *some* contribution to policymaking is assumed, as in the present case, then the nature of that contribution must be determined before its implications for the discipline can be examined. The analytic framework used to link discipline to policymaking must therefore be broad enough to allow determination of both the empirical and the normative requirements of reasoned policymakng.

The framework required is supplied here by a theory of knowledge. The products of economic inquiry are reasonably construed as knowledge, or claims to knowledge; the requirements for defensible and corrigible policy can also be stated in terms of specific kinds of knowledge. If a theory of knowledge is developed in which those statements intersect accurately, both the contribution that economics can presently make to reasoned policymaking and the changes required before economics can make a greater contribution to policymaking can be determined. The required theory of knowledge will differ very significantly from the epistemologies taught in philosophy. For one thing, the structure must be able to account for successful intellectual performance in disciplines whose performance is exceptional—notably the physical sciences and fields such as medicine or agriculture. The ultimate justification for accepting the theory of knowledge, and the concept of policy established within that theory, is the results obtained from acceptance and use. But reasons for agreeing to the theory of knowledge can be offered prior to use in any particular case, just as reasons can be offered for expecting a rocket to fly before it is actually launched. That is the function of methodology, or philosophy of inquiry.

## THE STRUCTURE OF THE ARGUMENT

The outline followed in the development of the argument is largely determined by its purpose. The theory of knowledge, which provides the overall framework in which the meaning of terms and the requirements for policymaking can be identified, is elaborated first (chapter 2). Then, a meaning is established for *policy* and *policymaking,* consonant with current usage but precise enough to allow specification of the necessary conditions for reasoned and corrigible policymaking (chapter 3). The contribution that the sciences can make to reasoned policymaking, specified in terms of knowledge produced, is examined in chapter 4. The goal there is to identify the necessary conditions for reasoned policymaking and show how they can be satisfied, using the framework supplied by the theory of knowledge. That set of requirements provides a base for assessing the contribution that contemporary economics can make to reasoned and corrigible policy (chapter 5). In the conclusion (chapter 6) I suggest some major changes that would have to be made before the products of economic inquiry could be used by a competent policymaker and outline some of the reasons why they seem unlikely to occur.

For the very generalized type of criticism undertaken here, only the more salient features of the economic paradigm need be identified. They are the principal headings in the major economic texts, the basic set of concepts and relations used in teaching economics and expanding economic knowledge. The central feature of the paradigm, the concept that ties together the various elements, is the "economic system," an analytic construct that serves as the focus of economic inquiry. The principal concern is with the exchange of goods and services within such economic systems through another analytic structure identified as the "market." Economists focus on various dimensions of the economic system, and they differ profoundly about the relative importance of various features of the system in the operation of the whole—as well as about the role that government can and should play. But concern for the economic system identifies the economist, and the concepts used to describe the elements in the system, identify processes, and project outcomes are shared by virtually all economists. Further, the basic procedure in economic inquiry, again shared by nearly all economists, is to develop a formal pattern or model that can explain or predict the operation of the system as a whole (macroeconomics) or some part of it (microeconomics). The strategy to be followed when producing such models, and their cognitive status when completed, is much disputed among economists. But the products of inquiry tend to be similar in form, and to perform the same functions, regardless of origin.

No other social science has developed a common paradigm of the type found in economics, though an effort was made in political science in the 1950s to gain acceptance for a unifying construct labeled the "political system."[7] Indeed, none of the physical sciences employs a paradigm analogous to the one that economists use. The structure is unique. The closest historical approximation to the economic system is the solar system that appears in astronomy. The economic system is expanding and growing more complex in a way that sets it apart from the solar system but the basic treatment of the two constructs within the respective disciplines is remarkably similar. That may not be mere coincidence. Economics has remained remarkably consistent in its approach to inquiry for nearly two centuries and the early economists were much influenced by the Newtonian conception of science, and in ways that current conceptions of science would scarcely allow. Some of the major impediments to using economics in reasoned policymaking are probably due to the influence of that underlying conception of the scientific enterprise.

Most economists share a common paradigm and a common approach to inquiry. The discipline is nevertheless extremely heterogeneous. There are some few areas in economics seriously concerned with applications and the knowledge produced there is usually adequate for use in reasoned policymaking. Agricultural economics, and to a lesser extent labor economics, illustrate the exceptions. For reasons best left to the historian, agricultural economics developed along different lines than the main body of economics, though the differences have decreased in the past two or three decades. Close ties with individual agricultural producers and mutual concern for improved production apparently provided the early agricultural economist with a "corn patch by proxy" against which the knowledge claims generated within the discipline could be tested. Whatever the reasons, the kinds of questions asked, the research designed to answer them, and the relation between economic evidence and findings and real world experience amply justified using the products of agricultural economics in policymaking or action. Clearly, the generalized criticism of economics developed here will not apply to such specialized areas.

To minimize controversy about the usefulness of particular economic studies, the research design followed here includes three important restrictions. First, the present inquiry is limited very strictly to an examination of the use of economic knowledge in reasoned policymaking. Second, the subfields in economics included in the study are identified as accurately as possible so that the reader will know the basis of the judgments made. Third, the critical apparatus is elaborated enough to allow the reader to apply it independently and thus obtain a test of the judgments made as well as a test of the critical apparatus.

The decision to limit the discussion to the usefulness of economics in policymaking rests mainly on the overriding importance of policymaking in contemporary society. Some of the implications of that restriction are worth further emphasis. First, to deny that economics is useful for policymaking does not require the claim that it has no uses whatever; at the very least, some economists have profited mightily from their work. Second, the validity of economics as an academic discipline is not disputed. (For the record, I see no way to create a viable social science or physical science on an other-than-pragmatic base, but that is a separate question.) Third, no distinction is made between so-called pure and applied science. Although it is accepted as a matter of course by both physical and social scientists, it has no persuasive basis in epistemology or methodology. That is, the distinction usually made between science and engineering is not predicated on differences in logical requirements, mode of inquiry, character of findings, or standards of test and argument. In most cases, usage seems to depend upon the way in which the purposes of inquiry are stated rather than the kinds of results anticipated or the assumptions on which those anticipations depend. For those who insist on the distinction, the goal here is a "philosophy of engineering" rather than a "philosophy of science." Fourth, the question, Is economics really a science? need not be raised. Whether economics is the "most scientific" of the social sciences or the most prestigious form of contemporary academic scholasticism is left for others to decide. The sole purpose here is to determine whether or not the products of economics are sufficient for reasoned policymaking, to provide the reasoning on which that judgment depends, and to draw the implications for the future contained in the findings. That overall focus allows for close analogies with medicine or agriculture where experience with applied knowledge has a long and successful history; illustrations and examples will be taken mainly from well-established cases in such fields.

Two minor points: first, to state that much of economics cannot be used for policymaking is not to deny that individual economists have contributed, and will contribute, to that end. There is enormous variation within the discipline. Second, criticism of economics implies no superiority on the part of other social sciences. So far as policymaking is concerned, there is little reason to prefer one over the others. The common assumption that economics has reached a level of power and precision not available in the other social sciences does, however, suggest that the *need* for criticism is greater in economics than in other fields.

Taken literally, the task of examining the products of economics in terms of their usefulness for reasoned policymaking far exceeds human capacity. The scope and volume of published material is immense. A detailed exploration of the materials listed in just one volume of the *Journal of Economic Literature* would be a major undertaking; four such volumes appear each year. The range of topics, techniques, and theses confounds efforts to develop an adequate sampling base. In calendar year 1979, for example, the *Journal* contained some 11,500 classifications of articles and 1,150 classifications of books. Each article or book could appear under several headings, depending on content. The distribution of publications by topic is shown for 1979 in the table. The figures have been rounded and are meant to do no more than suggest the overall distribution of effort within the profession, or more precisely, within the subclass of professional members who published in that year.

In terms of the *Journal*'s classification scheme, the nature and influence of the basic economics paradigm are most clearly seen in four areas: general economics, theory, and history; economic growth and planning; quantitative data and methods; and domestic monetary and fiscal policy. Approached from the other side, from policymaking requirements rather than economic production, the primary needs are for valid theories (the meaning of *theory* to be determined in chapter 2) and accurate predictions. They usually appear in the categories just enumerated. For practical reasons, the study concentrates on major figures in economics, on major texts or monographs, and on the major journals where theoretical and other articles relating to these four areas appeared. The books and collections used in the study are listed in the Bibliography. Each issue of four journals was examined for the period 1970-1980: *American Economic Review, Journal of Political Economy, Econometrica,* and *Journal of Post-Keynesian Economics.* One-fourth

**Types of Economic Publications: 1979**

| TOPIC | NO. OF ARTICLES | NO. OF BOOKS |
|---|---|---|
| General economics, theory, history | 1,900 | 260 |
| Economic growth, planning | 1,100 | 160 |
| Quantitative data, methods | 700 | 50 |
| Domestic monetary and fiscal theory | 1,600 | 100 |
| International economics | 1,000 | 115 |
| Administration, business, finance | 700 | 70 |
| Industrial organization | 900 | 75 |
| Agriculture, natural resources | 1,300 | 115 |
| Manpower, labor, population | 1,300 | 95 |
| Welfare, consumer and urban economics | 1,200 | 110 |

SOURCE: *Journal of Economic Literature* XVII, nos. 1-4 (1979).

18  Economics and Policymaking

to one-half of the issues produced during that decade by the following journals were also sampled: *Bell Journal of Economics, Cambridge Journal of Economics, Economic Inquiry, Economic and Social Measurement, Economic Journal, International Economic Review, Journal of Economic Issues, Journal of Economic Theory, Journal of Mathematical Economics, Journal of Public Economics, Journal of Urban Economics, Oxford Bulletin of Economics and Statistics, Quarterly Journal of Economics,* and *Regional Science and Urban Economics.*[8] My conclusions are based on a systematic examination of the contents of these journals and books. The overall approach to inquiry that appeared in the sample, examined from the perspective of the policymaker, should reveal enough of the performance of economics to justify generalized criticism.

NOTES

1. Thomas S. Kuhn, *The Structure of Scientific Revolutions* (University of Chicago Press, 1962).

2. See for example, Gordon Tullock, *Private Wants, Public Means: An Economic Analysis of the Desirable Scope of Government* (Basic Books, 1970); James M. Buchanan and Robert D. Tollison, eds., *Theory of Public Choice: Political Applications of Economics* (University of Michigan Press, 1972); Stuart Plattner, ed., *Formal Methods in Economic Anthropology* (American Anthropological Association, 1975). For the assumptions involved, see Dennis C. Mueller, *Public Choice* (Cambridge University Press, 1979), p. 1, "Public choice can be defined as the economic study of nonmarket decisionmaking, or simply as the application of economics to political science."

3. Paul A. Samuelson, "What Economists Know," in *The Collected Scientific Papers of Paul A. Samuelson,* ed. Joseph E. Stiglitz (MIT Press, 1966), vol. 1, p. 211.

4. Kuhn, *Structure of Scientific Revolutions,* ch. 3.

5. Stanley Wong, "The F-Twist and the Methodology of Paul Samuelson," *American Economic Review* 63 (June 1973): 312 (hereafter cited as *AER*).

6. Wassily Leontief, "Theoretical Assumptions and Nonobserved Facts," *AER* 61 (March 1971): 25.

7. David Easton, *The Political System* (Alfred A. Knopf, 1953); idem, *A Systems Analysis of Political Life* (John Wiley, 1965).

8. The journals were not equally useful, of course. Selection was made after consultation with, and on the advice of, a small group of economists— a sample admittedly skewed by personal acquaintance with the author.

# 2     The Theory of Knowledge

The products of economic inquiry can be linked to the needs of the policy-maker through a generalized framework supplied by a theory of knowledge. However, that theory must satisfy conditions quite different from those imposed on the epistemologies treated in conventional philosophy.[1] For one thing, it must include all of the basic assumptions required to generate a body of useful knowledge, to the extent they are known. More importantly, it must function as a genuine theory, in the full scientific sense of the term, and the theory itself must be testable in use over time, be open to improvement out of experience. The key to developing such a theory is the assumption that human actions are criticized and improved *only* by reference to a purpose. Thus far, efforts to develop an alternative base for justifying and improving human performance have been fruitless. Without reference to a purpose, the kind of evidence and argument needed to justify or criticize performance simply cannot be identified. It follows that the purposes sought through the application or use of knowledge must be identified before the theory can be created. Those purposes must lie within human capacity yet somehow satisfy the basic human needs with reference to the environment—otherwise, the theory will be partial and inadequate. Once the purposes are specified, the structures and processes required for achieving them can be determined. The resulting apparatus is a very powerful tool for criticizing intellectual performance, a tool that is itself open to test in terms of the achievement made by using it. The human significance of the set of purposes must be demonstrated outside the theory of knowledge, but that poses no particular problems for theory or theorist.

Development of the theory of knowledge therefore begins by identifying and justifying a set of purposes to be achieved through the use of knowledge. The goal is the widest construction possible, limited only by human capacity, for the critical apparatus generated within the theory is limited strictly to efforts to achieve those purposes. Most significant dimensions of human affairs must be accessible through the selected set of purposes. Once purposes are identified, discussion can proceed to an examination of the instruments required for achieving them, the limitations to which those instruments are subject, and the kind of evidence required to justify their use. This chapter concludes with a brief examination of the implications of the theory of knowledge for the conduct of inquiry when the goal is usefulness in policymaking—with particular reference to economics.

## THE PURPOSES OF INQUIRY

The set of human purposes used as a base for creating a theory of knowledge is analytically equivalent to the set of human needs that can be satisfied by intellectual activity if the theory is accepted. Intellectual purposes and human needs are but two sides of the same coin. Ideally, the statement of needs and purposes should be both comprehensive and parsimonious. Maximizing the generality of the statement of purposes broadens applications, but it also increases the danger that human capacity may be transgressed. Each need or purpose must be bounded precisely enough to allow determination of the conditions to be satisfied before it can be achieved—the necessary and/or sufficient conditions of achievement. The selection of purposes cannot and need not exhaust the enormous variety of human interactions with an environment that includes other humans. But if a small selection of purposes suffices to deal with most significant human interactions with the environment, they also suffice to organize systematic inquiry, and provide the criteria needed to reject, justify, or improve the resulting knowledge claims.

The procedure to be followed is to begin with a set of human purposes and work backward to see how they can be fulfilled within the limits of human capacity. For the kind of theoretical development required here, that procedure is essential. The selection of purposes supplies a base for evaluating proposed theories of knowledge. The procedure leads to a statement of requirements that is more or less independent of current capacity or current conceptions of inquiry, and thus avoids one of the more common forms of the availability fallacy. The resulting theory of knowledge must survive three kinds of testing. First, it should account for what has been accomplished intellectually in the past, particularly in such areas as physical science; in other words, it must separate valid knowledge from "patent medicine." Second, it must provide a generalized critical base that can be used by any discipline seeking to generate useful and usable knowledge, and therefore be testable by reference to such use. Finally, the theory will suggest both substance and strategies for educating youth in ways that optimize intellectual performance, hence their performance is also a test of theoretical adequacy. The theory of knowledge developed here can, I believe, satisfy these requirements better than any of the available alternatives. And preliminary efforts to implement the theory of education at various academic levels have been very successful and will be explored further.

The characterization of the human condition in which the essential human needs or purposes are developed must be dynamic and ongoing. Humanity is caught in an unending flow of time, and the dynamic character of the human situation is both a source of problems and an aid to their solution. Because humans are profoundly and often adversely affected by events in the environment, human survival and improvement, which is the central goal of human action, requires some capacity to adjust the relations between individual and environment in a systematic and defensible way. The self may be modified to better fit the environment; the environment may be changed to suit the self. Both types of action are common. The capacity for making such adjustments may lie in the individual (as knowledge) or in the collectivity (as mores and folk-lore), but it cannot be dispensed with entirely.

The apparatus required to adjust self to environment or environment to self consciously and deliberately must be *created*. It is not inherited with the genes; it cannot be "discovered" in nature, Plato notwithstanding. The creative dimension of knowledge production may be left to evolution, of course, but that is humanly expensive because no learning is involved. Nature preserves "improvements" by killing those who fail to improve, and not by teaching them how to adjust. Deliberate improvement of knowledge, or intentional learning, is more efficient and humanly less expensive. It is well known that individuals create but the procedures involved defy formal specification—there is no scientific method that can guarantee results in the same way that procedures justify conclusions in logic. But if creativity cannot be formalized it can nevertheless be facilitated, if only by eliminating impediments. If the instruments needed to achieve essential purposes are known, and the reasons why those instruments perform adequately can be determined, the inquirer can at least "know what he is looking for" and learn the characteristics that his creations must have if they are to perform adequately.

Analytically, the purposes fulfilled in the process of adjusting relations between individual and environment can be reduced to three, and they seem to be exhaustive. First, the individual must be able to *anticipate,* to predict or forecast, either events that have not yet occurred (It will be very cold in the morning) or events that have occurred but have not been observed (Last night's snow has blocked the mountain pass). Such predictions are mainly useful for suggesting modifications of the self that will adjust the relation between individual and environment. By themselves, predictions cannot provide a sufficient basis for human action. Knowing that a road will be blocked does not suggest what action should be taken. Other tools are required. Nevertheless, a forecasting device is an invaluable intellectual tool, and seeking to create structures that can predict significant events is a worthy enterprise.

The second fundamental need is for some measure of *control* over future events—past events are beyond human capacity to change. Being able to control events makes it possible to adjust the environment to individual preferences. More specifically, the individual must be able to intervene deliberately and knowingly in order to bring about a specific situation or change, or inhibit some antici-pated event. The process is exemplified in countless everyday actions: an umbrella is carried to ward off rain; an antibiotic is injected to eliminate a serious infection; a child is vaccinated to prevent successful future attacks by a particular germ. Change may be induced or inhibited by a wide range of actions but the principle involved is the same in all cases.

The instrument used to control future events necessarily includes a causal assumption; it may incorporate either the necessary or the sufficient conditions for change to occur. In both cases, the struc-ture will imply an intervention strategy, a way of acting that will, in principle at least, produce or inhibit a particular change under specified conditions. The action may not be technologically feasi-ble but that does not invalidate the instrument. When the neces-sary conditions for an event to occur are known, the event can be prevented; if the sufficient conditions are known, the event can be produced if the technology is available. If the tilt of the earth vis-à-vis the sun could be altered, for example, the earth's climate would be changed. The fact that it cannot be done does not invali-date the assumption, which is derived from well-established theories. The necessary and sufficient conditions for events to occur are both logically and empirically independent; each can be known without the other. Knowing that oxygen is necessary for burning suggests that fire can be prevented or stopped by eliminating oxygen from the site. But it can be known that a match will start a fire without knowing the role that oxygen plays, and without knowing how to stop the process once it is set in motion. Each bit of knowl-edge, each set of relations, can be established independently of the other, and each may have use or value.

Given the knowledge required to control events, the human actor is still not in possession of a sufficient basis for reasoned action. The instruments used for controlling the environment, like those used to make predictions, must be applied in conjunction with yet another tool. Reasoned and corrigible action requires addi-tional (normative) knowledge—the ability to choose or express a preference and defend it systematically. A valid forecast does not suggest a line of action until it is combined with capacity to control; knowing how to produce a change does not inform the actor whether to produce it or not until a preference has been accepted. Action always and necessarily entails choice; they are analytically indistinguishable. And choice depends on a normative or value judgment, an expression of preference. The third fundamental need or purpose, then, is to *choose.*

Actually, the need to choose is a logical necessity given the capacity to control events. Action produces change or prevents it and change is the usual indicator of action. But that is analytically inadequate. To avoid confusion, choice must be defined in terms of the actor's capacity rather than in terms of what the actor does. The effects of not acting when the capacity to act is available are then analytically equivalent to the effects of positive action, and a choice is made in either case. The result of action or choice is necessarily a world that is in some way different than it would otherwise have been. Actions change the world. By producing a world that is different, the actor chooses the world produced. Such choices can be determined analytically, without reference to the intentions, awareness, or behavior of the actor. Only the actor's capacity to create change need be known. The consequences of action can always be described as one state of the world *rather than* another state within the range of available options. The substance of any particular choice is the full range of accessible future states, determined by theoretical projection of the effects of action. To bring choice or action under reasoned control, the available outcomes are compared systematically and reasons are offered for preferring one state to the others. The reasons generated by a comparison of outcomes serve to solve the particular case; that solution can be generalized to produce a priority system applicable to a class of cases; the priority system will force a particular choice in an appropriate situation; the result is a test of the priority system for it can be compared to the result anticipated from the use of other priorities. The details of structure and process required will be examined fully and systematically below.

The theory of knowledge is built around three basic human needs: to anticipate events, to control them, and to choose or act. They seem exhaustive, sufficient for maintaining and improving the human condition, but the claim does not have to be that strong. So long as they are necessary for dealing with significant dimensions of human life, a theory of knowledge able to deal with them effectively is essential. That theory provides a base for criticizing efforts to achieve the purposes and for arguing cogently that such efforts have failed or succeeded. And since the requirements for success can be identified within the theoretical framework, it provides a way of stating the goals of inquiry that should contribute positively to improved performance.

The connection between the theory of knowledge and the intellectual requirements for reasoned policymaking is made through the instruments and processes required for reasoned choice. The informal conception of policy as a guide to action, which serves to link systematic analysis to customary usage, can be given a very precise meaning in the context of reasoned choice. The relation between the empirical and the normative dimensions of inquiry, which must be established before the role that economics plays in policymaking can be criticized on reasoned and defensible grounds, is determined within the same framework. That is, an examination of the structures and processes required in reasoned choice can suggest a precise meaning for "policy" and indicate the conditions that defensible, corrigible policies must satisfy. The relation between empirical and normative inquiry depends on the amount and kind of interdependence appearing between the instruments needed to control and predict events and the instruments and processes required for reasoned choice. The central question that an adequate theory of knowledge must resolve can then be stated precisely: How can fulfillment of the three basic human needs or purposes be brought under reasoned control and made defensible and corrigible? More narrowly, what kinds of instruments must be produced, within what set of limiting conditions, before human needs or purposes can be satisfied? The goal is a conception of knowledge that is adequate as a basis for action, reliable, and corrigible out of experience—and within human reach. The theory must allow knowledge claims, which are assertions about the way in which the basic purposes can be fulfilled in the real world, to be justified *in advance* of application, and if that cannot be done, to show how the application can be structured to provide evidence for or against future use of the same instrument.

## LIMITING ASSUMPTIONS

The content of a theory of knowledge intended for use in real world affairs is very strongly influenced by the set of limiting conditions assumed with respect to human intellectual capacity. It is unlikely that every such assumption can be identified precisely, but some of the basic limitations are known and worth explicit statement. Most are commonplace and not disputed, but their implications for the concept of knowledge that is accepted, and for the conduct of systematic inquiry, are not always appreciated, particularly in social science.

First, and perhaps most important, the human individual is assumed to depend entirely on the sensory apparatus for information about the internal or external environment (or the person). Perceptions of the external world, including the self, are in all cases mediated by the central nervous system. It follows that observations refer only to sense perceptions and not to external reality directly. The implications of that situation are surprisingly extensive. For observation cannot be used to justify statements about reality because the content of a statement cannot be compared directly to reality—the latter is and will remain unknown. A correspondence theory of truth is thereby ruled out and some other basis for justifying propositions that relate to the external world, including so-called factual statements, must be found. The "hard facts" implied in everyday usage to be products of observation dissolve into problematic statements, assumed and justified by reference to observation. Of course, propositions supported by observations *could* be treated as statements about reality, but in that case the content of reality would depend on further assumptions whose validity would also be uncertain. Nothing would be added by such procedures beyond, perhaps, some measure of psychological satisfaction gained by accepting the deception. The validity and reliability of a proposition construed as a statement about reality would be no greater than the validity and reliability of a proposition based on simpler assumptions and supported by reference to observation. The "reality" assumption adds considerably to the danger of misinterpretation without providing any benefits.

The second major restriction on the human capacity to generate reliable knowledge (actually a corollary to the first) results from the dynamic character of the human situation. The observer lives in a flow of time at the juncture of past and future, *facing backward.* Every proposition based on or justified by direct observation refers to the past. For a perception-limited observer, the raw materials from which the instruments needed to fulfill human needs must be forged (the substance of human knowledge) are part of the past. Human life, however, is lived "in" the future to a surprising degree. Nothing can be done about the past except learn from it, or perhaps seek to disguise it in some way. The future is where human expectations are realized, where the effect of efforts to control events is actually felt, where the results of action appear, where the meaning and content of choice is made known, where the reaction to choice takes place. Knowledge must be built from materials that refer to the past; knowledge is used to satisfy human needs in the future. Shorn of philosophic verbiage, that is the crux of the induction problem, the logical dilemma that a theory of knowledge must resolve or evade.

These two basic limits on human capacity have very extensive implications for the effort to produce knowledge. They affect both the kinds of knowledge that can be produced and the way in which knowledge claims can be justified. The limitations accepted, there is nothing to study beyond the record of past human experience (though future experience can be structured and then examined once it becomes part of the past) and no reason for study beyond the contribution made to the human future. There is no tenable alternative to egocentrism with respect to the species for members of the human race. If humanity is not accepted as the measure of all things human, then humanity is left without a measure—and without any basis for action that allows correction and improvement. There is no possibility of developing and justifying a criterion for measuring human performance, empirical normative, on a base that is external to mankind. The value of human life is only an assumption, but it must be made or human life itself becomes problematic.

Under the circumstances, it is both appropriate and reasonable to identify "knowledge" with the various structures and processes required for satisfying human needs and purposes—for improving the human condition. The quality of the knowledge can then be measured against human potential using human judgment. A theory of knowledge dependent on some fundamental specification of human needs is the best that can be hoped for. Given the capacity of the intellectual system and the nature of the human condition, no absolute base can be found for human knowledge, empirical or normative. Knowledge must be defined in a way that is conditional, relative, and problematic.

The substance of such a theory of knowledge consists necessarily in a set of assumptions adequate to create and justify the various structures needed to satisfy fundamental purposes. Such structures, combined with experience, must in turn justify accepting and acting on propositions that reference the future in particular ways. In principle at least, the justification must be available prior to use.

Put in slightly different terms, evidence based on observation is always and necessarily stated in singular and particular terms, contained in propositions that refer to a specific time and place. References to the future, whether they refer to empirical or normative matters, require propositions that are not limited with respect to time and place, propositions that are general in form. Strictly speaking, a particular proposition cannot be applied, for application necessarily involves inference and nothing can be inferred from it. A particular proposition may not be compatible with another proposition, or with an inference from some general proposition, but that is a different point. Human experience must be generalized before it can be used. Indeed, the solution to a particular case must actually be generalized before it can be applied to the case it was developed to solve.

This approach to knowledge shows the centrality of the induction problem in its narrower and more manageable sense. The instrument required for achieving some human purpose will always be generalized. Therefore the justification for accepting or rejecting the instrument cannot consist in a simple logical inference from propositions justified by observation for the latter are singular and particular in form, and formal logic does not permit the deduction of general propositions from singular propositions. Indeed, the ultimate logical system, which is capable of self-re-creation (a Turing machine) would be inadequate for the task. Logic is simply a way of exploring content and no singular proposition can contain a general proposition. The dilemma is formal and there is no solution. It must therefore be evaded. A justification for general statements must be sought through other means. Since the induction problem is universal, it functions in physical science as well as social science or normative inquiry. Clearly, there must be some way of evading the problem, else how to account for the success of the physical sciences? The solution might be available only to physical science, of course, but some kind of solution there must be—that can be demonstrated on empirical and historical grounds. As it turns out, the evasion is general and holds for all fields of inquiry; the dilemma can be circumvented in both empirical and normative affairs, in both physical and social science, including, of course, economics. How that evasion can be achieved, how knowledge of the kind required as a basis for action can be produced and justified within the limits of human capacity, is the question to which the discussion must now turn.

## EVADING THE INDUCTION PROBLEM

The induction problem can be avoided, and human purposes in the environment satisfied reliably and accurately, by a deceptively simple process. A pattern of generalized relations, a formal logical structure comprising a set of axioms and definitions that relate a collection of symbols, is *assumed* to fit an observed situation. The formal structure is assumed to be an isomorph for some real world situation, to be identical in form, though not, perhaps, in detail. The pattern is a human creation, developed within an existing logic such as algebra or within a logic generated specifically for the purpose in hand. It consists essentially of a set of variables and the rules that relate their values. Whatever the source, the structure must be formally calculable. The assumption of isomorphism depends on a comparison of the set of relations observed in the environment with the set of procedures and relations that occur within the calculus. Assuming isomorphism serves to link the symbols and rules in the logic to observation and experience, using what are usually called transformation rules. The relations that appear within the pattern, including the effects of change, are then transferred to the observed world. The implications of accepting the assumption of isomorphism may include predictions or expectations that result from specific observations, the expected result of specific actions, the kinds of intervention strategies that can be used to control the flow of events, or the actions required by accepting a specified normative structure. In effect, the assumption harnesses the calculating power of logic, available nowhere else, to the results of observation. The structure can be used to deal systematically with the future. However, since it depends on assumed isomorphism, the application of the structure is always problematic, and it can only be used to deal with recurring events. But in an ongoing and repetitive universe, the quality of the instrument can be improved over time, and reasons can be offered for agreeing that an improvement has been made. Maintenance and improvement of the human condition are thereby made possible.

The initial assumption of isomorphism between pattern and observation is tested by acting on it. In the simplest case, the implications generated by the pattern can be compared to events actually observed. Experience gained in use or application can provide grounds for retaining, rejecting, or modifying the pattern—or limiting its applications. In effect, a knowledge claim produced within the pattern is justified in the first instance by reference to the logic; the claim must be a logical consequence of accepting the pattern. The pattern itself is justified by reference to the effects of use, or by reference to relevant experience contained in other established patterns. The logical fit between proposed knowledge and accepted knowledge is perhaps the most important single test to be passed. Reliable knowledge evolves out of an ongoing cyclic process that includes the creation of patterns, their application, observation of the results, evaluation, and modification or reinforcement for future use. The process works only with recurring events, but nonrecurring events could not in any case provide knowledge useful for dealing with future cases. Illustrations of the dynamics of the process are plentiful in agriculture or medicine. Improvements in knowledge evolve out of endless cycles of trial and error. Agricultural improvement in particular can be shown to depend on continuing cycles of plowing, planting, tilling, harvesting, consuming, and modifying assumptions in the light of human reaction to consumption. The essential element in evaluation is, of course, human consumption and reaction, though it is often ignored or overlooked in accounts of science or explanations of scientific improvement. Even in physics, informed human reaction to use is the ultimate justification for claims to knowledge. That base is easily obscured because the patterns in use are highly generalized and mathematicized and there may be several layers of abstraction between pattern and observation.

The reaction of informed users is the ultimate court of appeal for all knowledge claims, empirical or normative, in physical or social science. The point deserves special emphasis, for it is often overlooked. The best illustrations are found in physical science. The judgments of the scientific community, aware of both competing alternatives and the available evidence, are decisive when nearly unanimous, but only for the time being. If there is no consensus, the status of the claim remains indeterminate. All decisions are conditional, however, even if unanimous. That may not seem consonant with more dramatic notions of science as a precise, objective, and decisive enterprise but the dramatic image is merely distorted. Similarly, it may seem unlikely that empirical and normative knowledge depend on the same form of justification, but there is no viable alternative available. There is always room for differences in judgment or informed disagreement; such disagreements are more likely in normative affairs, or in social sciences such as economics, than in physics or chemistry. But the disagreements merely acknowledge that there are situations in which judgment must be withheld, temporarily at least, until more evidence is available. The judgment of evidence must be competent, which raises other problems, but the principle involved does not change.

Evasion of the induction problem requires three major assumptions that need explicit statement and examination. First, it must be assumed that humans can create, can transcend formal inferences and produce new patterns that are generalized in form and therefore contain *more than* the sum of their antecedents. Second, the individual must respond differentially to differences in the human situation, or express a preference for one situation rather than another. Third, the human situation must be ongoing in time, and some capacity for dealing systematically and reliably with events must already be available. Knowledge as a whole is treated incrementally and regarded as problematic. None of the three assumptions is open to serious dispute.

In the aggregate at least, human creativity is well documented. The individual human has demonstrated capacity for organizing or generalizing experience, for creating and using logical structures. There is neither magic nor mystery in the process of developing and applying knowledge. Logics consist in sets of symbols whose meanings are very precisely defined but in nominal or stipulative terms; they do not refer to anything in the world of experience. The relations among the symbols are stated exhaustively in the set of axioms included in the calculus. By accepting axioms and definitions, the individual is able to determine the implications of altering the structure in specified ways fully and perfectly. For example, when such terms as line, point, angle, and so on are adequately defined, as in geometry, and sets of axioms are postulated that suffice to define triangles, then the implications of those axioms (which include the characteristics of triangles) can be explored fully and formally within the calculus. The logical process actually functions by simple substitution; nothing is added to axioms or definitions. Logic, or mathematics, is tautological. Calculations are made only within such formal structures and the results apply only to the formal symbols. The application of logic to observation is a creative action; it does not have a logic, and cannot be formalized. Before applications are possible, reasons must be offered for assuming that elements of the observed world interact in the same way as elements in the logic, that the axioms of the logic fit the processes of the observed world. Merely fixing labels to logical symbols is not enough. If changes that occur within the logical structure are isomorphic to events that occur in the observed world, the structure can be used for predicting real world events. If a causal assumption between the variables in the structure can be justified, the instrument can be used to control events. The question whether or not a logical structure has been applied properly depends mainly on knowledge of the observable world rather than knowledge of logic. Indeed, logical training confers no special competence in the application of logic and in principle at least could be counterproductive. How decisions relating to the use of logic in everyday affairs can be made and criticized, and what the requirements entail for systematic inquiry aimed at policymaking, will be examined more fully below.

    The human capacity to react differentially to differences in the human condition, and to do so regularly and consistently, is also well established. The structures and processes required to bring that reaction under control and harness it to justification of choices are less commonly understood. Far more is involved than direct affective reaction. Indeed, an affective reaction is simply a fact in human experience, a condition that occurs unwilled and unsought. Reactions are observed by the person reacting, and can be reported to others; they can also be modified or even suppressed entirely. The link between affective reaction and behavior is subject to very extensive modification. That is the major difference between humans and other species, and it supplies a base for developing a defensible human ethics. The process that restrains the patient from harming the physician who causes pain during treatment has no parallel in the reactive system of ants; the process by which humans react affectively to acts of cruelty perpetrated against persons far removed from themselves sets them apart still more. Harnessing and organizing these uniquely human capacities provides a point of departure for justifying choices.

Finally, the ongoing character of the world in which we live and the availability of knowledge within that system are commonplace. Even the confirmed hermit did not begin life isolated from his kind—a point that survival confirms. Intellectually, there is no need to begin at ground zero in the manner of Descartes, which is extremely fortunate, for if mankind began with a blank slate, the last remaining human would have very little to write upon it and the intervening time span would be short. The human inheritance plays a vital role in a theory of knowledge. The quality of the various parts of the inheritance varies greatly: some knowledge claims are accurate and valuable, some are very weak or mistaken, some are spurious and even dangerous. But the overall inheritance is there, an essential ingredient in species survival. Perhaps the most important function of methodological inquiry is to provide means for assessing the quality of the various elements in the available knowledge supply. In particular, the principles incorporated into the intellectual constitution, the rules that guide the quest for knowledge or determine the goals of inquiry, require periodic reexamination in the light of the knowledge produced while they were in effect. As in politics, improvement in the rules that control the making of rules is likely to have a much greater impact on the human future than any decision made under those rules. There are limits to what can be accomplished by constitutional manipulation, of course, for its effects are primarily negative or preventative. And there can be no mechanical solution to intellectual problems, no method for generating knowledge automatically and reliably. But if some changes can be made in the current conception of the nature of knowledge, the characteristics of adequate and justifiable inquiry, and the kinds of criteria used to evaluate results, that would have a highly beneficial effect on the educational system and on policymaking—not least with respect to economic matters.

## THE LINK TO PHILOSOPHY

The theory of knowledge being developed here is by no means totally divorced from philosophy and its problems. Thus far, aspects of the theory of knowledge that are different from conventional philosophy have been stressed. Viewed from a broader perspective, however, the development of useful, reliable, and corrigible knowledge depends on a number of assumptions about the relations between individual and environment that are part of the common philosophic heritage. Taken as a whole, they serve to link the theory of knowledge to contemporary philosophy in a fairly useful way, particularly by suggesting the areas in which philosophers might greatly assist with the effort to anticipate and control events and make choices. The critical assumptions have to do with the relation between human perception and reality, with the nature of words and concepts and the way in which their meaning is developed, and with the ways in which claims to know can be tested and argued. In philosophic terminology, they are usually labeled empiricism, naturalism, instrumentalism, nominalism, and pragmatism. In philosophy, each doctrine may be regarded as an independent epistemology. Here, each is construed as part of the integrated structure required to satisfy human needs reliably and corrigibly. The assumptions are validated by their contribution to that end, compared to the contribution that might be expected if other assumptions were made. They have already been touched upon briefly in the foregoing discussion, though without philosophic labeling (to avoid needless argument about usage) and can therefore be treated briefly and summarily.

The assumption that human beings acquire information about the environment only through the sensory apparatus is commonly labeled *empiricism,* though in philosophy the connotations of the term usually extend beyond that limited meaning. Although empiricism implies that reality is beyond human reach, there are nevertheless good reasons for assuming that there is an external world, that "something is out there" which has stable characteristics.

That assumption allows use of the external environment as a limit or constraint on knowledge claims—the doctrine is known as *naturalism*. Accepting naturalism and empiricism forces rejection of both the idealist's claim to absolute knowledge and the mystic's claim to have obtained knowledge through transcendental channels. In effect, they divorce the criteria of acceptability applied to knowledge claims from assertions about the content of reality and thereby eliminate a correspondence theory of truth. The result is forced acceptance of pragmatic criteria of validity in knowledge.

In combination, empiricism and naturalism lead the inquirer to accept the doctrine known as *instrumentalism,* the assumption that human knowledge is best construed as a set of instruments or tools that can be used to fulfill human purposes. Knowledge, by implication, is created by organizing and generalizing past experience, by fitting experience to formal or logical patterns thus creating instruments that can serve specified purposes within stated limits. The test of such instruments, proximately at least, is success in achieving specific purposes. Ultimately, of course, the validity of the knowledge produced depends on human willingness to accept both purposes sought and the means used to achieve them in preference to any available alternative given full knowledge of the possibilities.

The fourth general assumption in the theory of knowledge is that the meaning of words, which are the carriers of knowledge claims, lies in the sets of conventions that define their use. No word, given that assumption, has any "real" or essential meaning, to be discovered in nature, as Plato among others suggested. The meaning of words depends on human intention; the words themselves are merely labels or symbols. That doctrine, called *nominalism,* avoids endless arguments about the "real" meaning of words, and about the propositions in which they are employed. More important, it brings that aspect of inquiry under reasoned control and reinforces the assumption that systematic inquiry is a creative process and not an expedition seeking to discover knowledge or truth. To use a phrase coined by Karl Popper, nominalism implies that the meaning of terms is defined from "right to left," that meaning is determined first and the label is appended afterward, so the inquirer does not begin with a term and seek its "essential," or "true" meaning. Modest though it may appear, that procedure of defining terms from right to left has had a significant impact on traditional philosophic speculation and would produce some highly salutory effects within economics if adopted and enforced.

Taken together, empiricism, naturalism, instrumentalism and nominalism, construed in the very limited sense used here, force humanity to deal with the world out of its own resources and capacities. Both the goals sought through the use of knowledge, and the knowledge used to achieve them, are human creations, tested against human criteria of adequacy. The search for knowledge, the impetus to inquiry, is best construed as a quest for a set of working assumptions, tentatively held, that are acceptable in the light of experience and adequate for the purpose in hand. The purpose sought is developed and evaluated in precisely the same manner. Such a context forces reliance upon a *pragmatic test of knowledge claims,* and therefore requires that knowledge be stated in a form amenable to pragmatic testing. Again, there is no alternative available if the overall purpose of knowledge is to guide actions in ways that maintain and improve the human situation. The "truth" of empirical and normative propositions cannot be established. But the accuracy and reliability with which specified purposes can be achieved under stated conditions using particular instruments can be assessed. That is the pragmatic criterion in a nutshell. Pragmatism does not solve all of the problems incident to development of knowledge, obviously, but it does provide a working principle that can lead to improvement in an ongoing enterprise, and provide reasons for arguing that an improvement has been made, and that the enterprise is worth continuing.

The need for the kind of evaluative criteria that pragmatism can supply is particularly noticeable in disciplines such as economics when they seek to provide assistance for policymaking. The extent to which conflicting and inconsistent economic knowledge is claimed by experts of equal repute on matters of vital importance is often remarked. The evidence for the available body of economic knowledge varies enormously; the criteria of inquiry and evaluation employed within the discipline are often disparate. The practice of testing instrument against purpose provides a workable base for making qualitative judgments of achievements within economics, as in other disciplines. And vigorous enforcement of quality control is the key to improvement. The ability to differentiate science from patent medicine, ritual from research, or magic from legitimate prediction is absolutely essential; the difference itself will always be relative. Thus damning insects with bell, book, and candle is one way of dealing with them; applying a dose of insecticide is another. Neither is absolutely superior; without reference to purpose, qualitative differentiation is impossible. Given a purpose, the assessment is easy. If the aim is to eliminate insects, the insecticide is preferable to prayer; if the aim is to demonstrate piety, the other preference holds.

The quality of any tool can be assessed by relating it to purpose; indeed, the quality of a tool cannot be stated apart from some purpose. The relative worth of two or more tools is evaluated by comparing performance of some common task. No absolute, external criterion is either possible or required. The fabled judge in a singing contest who heard the first finalist and promptly awarded the prize to the second implies a criterion of evaluation that is tempting but not humanly attainable. For intellectual purposes, relative standards are adequate, which is fortunate because absolute standards cannot be created on reasoned and defensible grounds. In the theory of knowledge, instruments are created for use and tested against their ability to generate reliable and accurate expectations, to control events adequately for the achievement of purpose, or to produce the preferred outcome in an appropriate choice situation. The purposes used to test specific instruments are themselves testable using precisely the same procedures. That is, the situation produced by accepting one purpose is compared to the situations that could have been produced by accepting one of the available alternatives, seeking reasons for maintaining or modifying the set of purposes currently being employed. Though complex, the task of justifying relative preferences is much easier than that of developing absolute, external evaluation criteria. Of course, there are unavoidable limits to human capacity for exploring alternatives. But comparisons made systematically open the way to developing new purposes, and new means for achieving them; they provide launching pads for further experiments in the development of knowledge. Not every launch will be fruitful, but every launch has that potential. The process will suffice for maintaining, improving, and expanding the knowledge system, and thereby satisfying the needs of the human population with increasing effectiveness and efficiency while improving the quality of the justification offered for selecting the expressed needs that are being satisfied.

The theory of knowledge sketched very briefly in this chapter is but one way of approaching the problem. There are many competitors. None is equally effective if the goal is knowledge that can direct human action. A simple process of creating, assuming, applying, and reacting can lead to the kinds of modifications needed to improve the knowledge supply. The conception of knowledge and inquiry that emerges fits the patterns of scientific inquiry, accounts for the success of intellectual efforts where they have been successful, notably in physical science, and suggests means for improvement where success has been limited. Moreover, the theory can also account for success in less likely areas, such as athletics, education, public administration, or even the arts. Knowledge so conceived is necessary for survival and within human capacity. The same set of structures and processes can serve both empirical and normative needs. Indeed, the two aspects of inquiry are firmly integrated, for the structure develops from the normative *to* the empirical. The substance of empirical inquiry is determined by normative need. The theory is readily transmitted to others and applied by them, in quite diverse fields. And the theory is testable, both against the achievements of science and through education. The performance of those educated to adjust their actions on the basis of self-conscious assessment of situational requirements developed with the use of the critical apparatus provides direct evidence of the overall acceptability of the theory.

## NOTE

1. For a full and detailed statement of the epistemological position, see Eugene J. Meehan, *Reasoned Argument in Social Science: Linking Research to Policy* (Greenwood Press, 1981) or idem, *The Foundations of Political Analysis* (Dorsey Press, 1971). For comparison with other approaches to epistemology or theory of knowledge, particularly in philosophy of science, see the following: Hubert M. Blalock, Jr., *Theory Construction: From Verbal to Mathematical Formulations* (Prentice-Hall, 1969); Richard B. Braithwaite, *Scientific Explanation: A Study of the Function of Theory, Probability, and Law in Science* (Harper and Brothers, 1960; Herbert Feigl and May Brodbeck, eds., *Readings in the Philosophy of Science* (Appleton-Century-Crofts, 1949); Paul K. Feyerabend, "Philosophy of Science: A Subject with a Great Past," in *Historical and Philosophical Perspectives of Science,* ed. Roger H. Stuewer, Minnesota Studies in the Philosophy of Science, vol. 5 (University of Minnesota Press,

1970); George Gale, *Theory of Science: An Introduction to the History, Logic, and Philosophy of Science* (McGraw-Hill, 1979); Norwood R. Hanson, *Patterns of Discovery* (Cambridge University Press, 1958); Carl G. Hempel, *Aspects of Scientific Explanation and Other Essays in the Philosophy of Science* (Free Press, 1965); Ernest Nagel, *The Structure of Science: Problems in the Logic of Scientific Explanation* (Harcourt, Brace and World, 1961); Ernest Nagel and Richard B. Brandt, eds., *Meaning and Knowledge: Systematic Readings in Epistemology* (Harcourt, Brace and World, 1965); Karl R. Popper, *The Logic of Scientific Discovery* (Science Editions, 1961); idem, *Objective Knowledge: An Evolutionary Approach* (Oxford University Press, 1972); Stephen Toulmin, *The Philosophy of Science: An Introduction* (Harper and Row, 1960); idem, *Human Understanding,* vol. 1, *The Collective Use and Evolution of Concepts* (Princeton University Press, 1972).

# Policymaking and
## 3 ———— Reasoned Choice

To assess the contribution that economics
can make to policymaking, the meaning
of *policy* must be established in a context that allows specification of the
requirements that a defensible and
corrigible policy must satisfy. The
context is supplied by the theory of
knowledge. The point of departure is
found in the everyday meaning of
policy as a guide to action. Within the
theory of knowledge, action is analytically equivalent to choice. The
discussion therefore proceeds by elab-
orating the concept of choice in ways
that demonstrate the structures and
processes involved in making and
defending reasoned choices. If the
meaning of policy can be located within
that structure without distorting contemporary usage, the critical apparatus
available within the theory can be
transferred to real world affairs. That is,
if some structure can be found within
the requirements for reasoned choice
that is accurately characterized as a
"guide to action," it can be identified
with the term policy, thus creating
the needed link to the critical apparatus.
The concept of policy that emerges
from this line of inquiry will not fit
every case of common usage, of course,
but it should correspond fairly well

with the meaning accepted in some of the better developed areas of policymaking, notably foreign relations. So long as the definition is not idiosyncratic, it can safely be accepted; usage is far too diverse to require more. At the present time, there is no conception of policy available that is adequate for systematic criticism. The goal, therefore, is to develop an adequate meaning for the term and provide reasons for accepting and using it.

Analytically, systematic criticism of choices or actions is much facilitated, and the difficulties often encountered in efforts to deal with failure to act or nonaction can be avoided, if choice or action is defined by reference to human potential—the actor's capacity to produce change in the environment—rather than by overt behavior. In other words, once an actor has been identified and the situation specified, the different outcomes that lie within the actor's capacity can be projected by appropriate theories. That set of outcomes makes up the content of the choice to be made. The capacity to produce change may be exercised by inaction as well as positive action. In either case, the result is a world in some way different than it would have been had the actor chosen differently. Allowing the drift course of events to flow on unimpeded when the capacity to intervene effectively is present is as much an action as direct intervention. In both cases, the choice made involves the same set of alternatives or outcomes, and is therefore subject to the same criticisms.

Conceptually, action is determined by capacity and situation. Given adequate instruments, the outcomes that lie within an actor's capacity can be projected on the future with some degree of reliability. The actor's potential depends on capacity and situation; the choice is substantively independent of either intention or awareness on the actor's part. The psychological dimensions of action can be ignored by the critic unless the focus of criticism is the actor and not the action. Where there is a genuine capacity to produce change, some choice is made. That choice has consequences: the world is in some way different than it would otherwise be. The usage may at times sound peculiar but it avoids some very serious conceptual difficulties. Within the theory of knowledge, capacity forces choice. In that limited sense, science (which is essentially capacity to act) actually *requires* mankind to be moral by forcing choice, and science is one of the prerequisites to morality because of the need to project the set of outcomes from which a choice is made. Action or choice forced by capacity cannot be avoided by choosing to do nothing; and the problem cannot be solved by choosing everything because there are scarcities. Capacity is limited.

The actions that produce change need not be physical. Indeed, actions that influence the lives of large numbers of persons are unlikely to be direct and physical if such special cases as the explosion of atomic weapons are excluded. Large populations are most readily and extensively affected by indirect actions, particularly through collectivities—transfer of resources or modifications in the existing set of legal rights and obligations, for example. Physical action is important in direct interpersonal relations rather than collective affairs. Social actions may have physical consequences for the individual, of course, but that is another matter.

Since choices can be made without either intention or awareness on the actor's part, it follows that not every action or choice is reasoned and defensible. But some part of the total set of human actions involves a deliberate effort to weigh alternatives, to compare them systematically by reference to some structured conception of benefits and costs. That subclass will be identified as *reasoned* choices; members of the subclass are in principle corrigible. The definition of reasoned choice is deliberately made weak and easily satisfied; all that is required is a weighing of alternatives. The quality of the process followed or instruments used may vary greatly. That is, options may be ignored, calculations may be mistaken, costs may be suppressed, or measurements may be inaccurate. But the act of consciously weighing and comparing necessarily entails development of certain kinds of structures and acceptance of some set of assumptions. Those structures and assumptions allow the actor to give reasons for a particular choice. If they do not suggest reasons for preference, the choice is a matter of indifference. Giving reasons, however weak or faulty, establishes the essential base for improving choices. That is, criticism of action or choice refers necessarily to the reasons that can be offered for or against a particular choice; it does open the choice to further discussion and argument and therefore to improvement. Given the present state of social theory and ethics, establishing a process that makes improvement possible at least in principle is the primary intellectual requirement.

The content of any choice is the sum of all the options available to a specified actor at a given time and place. Each option is efficiently expressed as a descriptive account of the world that will be produced if that choice is made. The range of choices closely resembles a set of film clips of the future, projected by an appropriate instrument and triggered by action. The actor can choose one film clip; *all* of the events in the clip must be accepted. Choice is bounded on the one hand by necessity and on the other hand by impossibility, neither of which is an object of choice. The critical framework deals only with human choices, not with evaluation of actors or of the effects of natural events. An earthquake may produce the same result as a war but the war is a human action and open to criticism while the earthquake is not. The consequences of choice are always stated in the form, "Outcome A *rather than* outcomes B, C, . . . N." Since each choice actually produces the preferred outcome in a situation, it reifies the normative apparatus on which it depends. But the normative system cannot be inferred from the choice: any number of priority systems may lead to the same outcome, depending on the way in which the choice is conceptualized. Since outcomes lie in the future, they are projected and not observed, therefore they are always problematic. The risk attached to each option, the likelihood that the outcome will appear, may play an important part in reasoned choices.

Choices are corrected and improved over time in the same way as efforts to predict or control events. Human experience with the set of outcomes from which a choice is made are organized and generalized into patterns (here called priorities) that serve as instruments of choice. Accepting the pattern forces a particular choice. When that occurs, the results of choice serve to test the pattern, or provide evidence for maintaining or modifying the pattern. As in other areas of human activity such as agriculture or medicine, the human reaction to living with the results produced by accepting the pattern, in full knowledge of the experiences associated with the alternatives, is the ultimate court of appeal in case of dispute. Reasoned choice combines the human capacity for differential affective response with the human capacity for modifying affective reactions on cognitive or intellectual grounds. Usually, that involves an extension of the implications of choice to wider time frames or to include the social or collective implications of individual action. Individual action has a social dimension in two senses:

the society may intervene to alter the costs and benefits attached to the various options; choosing an option implies choosing a society that both generates the option and allows it to be chosen. Individual exercise of free options within social bounds provides the evidence used to modify or retain those boundaries. The details of structure and process are examined in the remainder of this chapter. The goal is an adequate statement of the instruments required for reasoned choice or action which in turn will permit an unambiguous and persuasive formulation of the concept of policy.

## STRUCTURES AND PROCESSES IN REASONED CHOICE

The basic elements in reasoned choice are straightforward and uncontroversial. At a minimum, there must be an actor, an action, a situation in which action occurs, and a range of at least two achievable options. Every action has an empirical and normative dimension. Empirically, the content of the choice must be determined; normatively, a structure is needed that can identify the preferred outcome. Serious criticism of human actions will necessarily refer to both of these dimensions.

### THE FOCUS OF CRITICISM

In principle, systematic criticism of choice could focus on the qualities of the actor, the nature of the action, or the consequences of action.[1] However, the use of either actor or action as a critical base can be ruled out. Criticism addressed to the qualities of the person has by now been so thoroughly discredited in secular ethics that further argument is not needed. It is often useful, or even essential, to know the actor's intentions or purposes, but only if the aim is to criticize the actor. Intentions cannot be used as a focus for criticism without risking anomaly and inconsistency. Common purposes are successfully pursued by widely divergent means; actions seeking divergent purposes may produce identical outcomes. Criticizing the action by reference to the actor turns out to be unworkable. A parallel problem arises when actions are criticized by their intrinsic properties. Criteria for evaluating, or even identifying, those intrinsic properties have proved elusive. And "rule" ethics face the same problem if they are judged by their intrinsic character. On the other hand, if a rule is judged by its consequences, applying a fixed rule to variable circumstances produces mixed outcomes and inconsistency. No effort to base evaluation of action on the qualities of the actor or on the properties of the action has survived application to human affairs, or even succeeded in dealing with human affairs.

A useful basis for criticizing action can be developed by focusing on the consequences of action—comparing results actually produced with the available alternatives. The actor must be identified, but only to allow the options to be determined accurately. It is well known that individual capacity varies, even with respect to the occupants of major public offices. Once the content of a choice is projected, comparison of the outcomes supplies a basis for criticism. The side effects of action are already included in the projection of outcomes and require no special attention. A choice is reasoned if it involves some systematic comparison of outcomes, leading to reasons for preferring one to the others. Once reasons are offered for making a choice, improvement over time through argument becomes possible in principle. Willingness to explore the alternatives and their implications, given knowledge and competence, will eventually bring all of the available evidence and argument into the particular choice. Such a course of action does not guarantee agreement, but it does serve to clarify the locus of disagreement, thereby opening the way to resolving it.

The justification offered for preferring one outcome to another will depend on the situation. But the reasons can be found only in prior human experience with the various situations from which a choice is made. If there has been no prior experience with a situation, actions may be arranged to provide that experience and thus generate a basis for future improvements. The reasons themselves consist ultimately of statements about the quality of human life within the different circumstances from which a choice is to be made. What constitutes the most compelling reason for preferring one outcome to another is determined by the judgment of fully informed persons. There can be serious disagreements about preference. They may be resolved by further development and analysis, by incorporation of additional considerations, or they may remain unresolved. The process of normative development is likely to be very slow, other things equal, and there can be no guarantee that every difference, or even every significant difference, can be solved. However, there is also no reason to believe that every issue will end with fundamental disagreement or conflict. Articulation of the argument at least opens the way to further exploration of its quality. The position is weak, but it exhausts the human capacity to deal with choice on reasoned grounds. There is no promising alternative in sight.

More positively, the approach outlined above offers some definite advantages to individual and society. First, it requires no more than the capacity to give *some* reason for choice or preference. External criteria of judgment, or an absolute preference scale, are not required. Choices are resolved by a comparison of particular outcomes. The question, Is A preferable to B? is much more easily answered than the question, Should I do A? or Is A a good thing? Further, the procedure calls attention to the costs of action, the alternatives sacrificed to obtain the preferred outcome. In addition, only those choices that actually recur need be solved. It would be difficult to solve choices before they appear, and pointless to seek solutions to nonrecurring choices. The approach also avoids the tendency to universalize rather than generalize solutions to particular decisions. All that is required is a preference pattern that can handle most of the cases in a class; the structure need not function perfectly. Normative discussion has for too long been frustrated by efforts to handle both the everyday problem and the exceptional case within a single structure. The "Caligula syndrome," the effort to deal with the moral monster by the same rules used to handle everyday problems facing ordinary people, is unnecessary—Caligula can be dealt with *ad hoc*.

The procedure used to make choices parallels the procedure used to develop forecasts or instruments for controlling the environment. Choice begins with the particular case, as the search for theory begins with a particular phenomenon, analytically if not historically. The particular case is resolved by comparing available alternatives; the solution is generalized and can then be applied and tested. In effect, experience is organized into patterns which convert the outcome of comparisons into forced actions. Over time, normative solutions to recurring problems can be generalized further, and integrated, as in empirical theorizing, but that may not occur and there is no way to be certain that creative action will take place when it is needed. The collection of priority systems in use makes up the ethic of the individual or the society. Each such ethic is incomplete and only partially integrated. Many will contain serious lacunae, inconsistencies, or contradictions. Taken in conjunction with the generally poor theoretical capacity of the social sciences, the uncertain quality of the priority structures in use creates a major problem for the critic of policy. It is often impossible to determine whether the source of policy differences lies in the conception of policy accepted by the protagonists, the empirical structures used to project the available outcomes, or the priority system applied to them. Since locating the source of disagreement is prerequisite to resolving it, much work in the sociology of values is likely to be needed before policymaking can be placed on a sound empirical-normative foundation. Criticism based on the broad characteristics of the instruments used, however, need not await that development.

STRUCTURING THE OUTCOMES

The simplest choice involves a single actor, a specified situation, and two outcomes which differ in only one significant respect. It may never occur in the real world. In principle, the actor may be an individual or a collectivity since the procedures involved are the same in either case. But collective actors pose some special hazards for the critic. Individual choice usually begins with an identified actor. Most collective actions begin instead with a situation in the environment that requires change. In such cases, the first step is to locate an actor able to deal with the situation. If there is none, the collective authority may be able to create such an actor and resolve the difficulty. If there are several agents able to produce the required change, the costs are likely to differ. Some mechanism is then needed to rationalize the choice of actors and optimize benefits and costs. If both A and B can perform action X, but A will not because his priorities require doing Y and the cost of having action X performed by B is twice the cost of having it done by A, benefits remaining constant, the social costs of the decisioning machinery in force are probably excessive. Further, agencies such as Congress or Parliament created to exercise collective authority usually make decisions by aggregating particular individual choices through a set of formal rules. As has often been noted, it may not be possible to assign responsibility for such collective actions to any individual or group, hence the range of options actually available may be indeterminate. Since the aggregating procedure may convert defensible individual choices into a collective disaster, that characteristic has some extremely important implications for society and individual alike. These vital issues have been extensively discussed elsewhere and are not considered here.[2]

For any human individual, life is quite accurately depicted as an endless series of decision points. Choices are made, or actions are taken, at each point. Most of these decisions are ignored in everyday life, which may be essential for preserving sanity within the species. For example, the person who goes to a store for a pack of cigarettes does not usually weigh the alternative uses that could be made of the resources involved. Yet the choice is real, and the choice is made when the action is taken. Allowing events to flow uninterrupted, or socializing large populations to ignore certain available options for individual or society, could be a poor strategy in some circumstances. In periods of rapid social change, the socialization process that alerts the individual to crucial decisions may be hopelessly inadequate, just as the individual who changes cultures may find that social patterns brought from the previous culture are inadequate or counterproductive in the second.

In principle, a reasoned choice can be made at any decision point. What actually moves the person to weigh costs and benefits systematically in one case but not in others lies beyond the scope of the inquiry, but it poses major problems for social psychologists and for societies. Analytically, any decision node offers an opportunity to choose on reasoned grounds. Since a decision *is* made at each such point, once choice has been identified with capacity rather than action, the structures and processes developed for making reasoned choices must apply to any situation the individual might encounter.

Viewed longitudinally, reasoned choice is a simple four-step procedure. The alternatives are projected by theory, reasons for preferring one outcome to the others are sought in experience, the solution is generalized and applied, and the results are monitored for evidence that can be used in future decisions. How the alternatives are structured tends to determine both the kind of evidence that is weighed and the justification offered for the decision. Since choices are made within the particular constraints provided by real situations, and cannot be made outside that context, general discussion cannot solve specific choices. But the structures and processes involved can be identified, and some of the problems and possibilities can be explored.

A human action triggers a chain of reactions just as a stone dropped into a river produces wave movement on the surface. In both cases, the results may be very difficult to identify and trace. The effects of action are a function of the type of action and the situation in which it occurs. Several instruments may be needed to probe the full effects of quite simple actions and thus specify the content of the available options. However powerful the available theories, the results are always incomplete and in some degree problematic—the theories used in projection, and the judgments involved, may fail. What is most striking about human choice is the speed with which the chain of consequences grows complex, and fades. By necessity rather than choice, humans live and choose very close to the present.[3]

Some capacity to project the consequences of action is clearly essential for reasoned policymaking. In the social sciences generally, that capacity is extremely limited. Part of the problem arises from a failure to pursue an identifiable purpose in the environment; part can be ascribed to the tendency for academics to demand too much of their products, overlooking the value of limited instruments. Any tool that can improve on random behavior may be used with profit in some situation if no better alternative is available. Much can be done with very weak tools if they can be corrected in use over time. Corrigibility is a function of structure, logic, and testing; success usually depends on the conception of inquiry and its purposes from which the tool is derived. The importance of building a learning component into established institutions and procedures increases almost on the inverse square with the power and usefulness of the available knowledge supply.

*The Normative Variables*   Reasoned choices are made from a set of outcomes projected on the future; the outcomes must be comparable in terms of their normatively significant dimensions. Since any situation can in principle be conceptualized in an infinite number of ways, a set of common denominators, here labeled *normative variables,* must be selected from those available—or created especially for that purpose. Otherwise, comparisons with respect to a common dimension of each outcome could not be made, arguments about choices would not intersect, and choice could not be improved. Since any factor may have normative significance, depending on circumstances, the central problem with the normative variables is to determine the relative importance to be assigned to each member of a given set. Fortunately, all human cultures provide a point of departure for identifying normative variables and weighting their importance, though some are more easily defended than others. Reasoned choice, or criticism of choice, will usually begin with the established normative apparatus, using both variables and priorities currently in use. However, each choice is in principle open to criticism by reference to any legitimate way of conceptualizing the outcomes. Indeed, the introduction of new normative variables is one major device for improving the scope, and therefore the quality, of an established ethic. That is, an ethical structure that includes concepts relating to the psychic states of individuals is an improvement on a structure that does not, other things equal. In the long run, the weight attached to a particular variable (which can change) is less important than a determined effort to take everything relevant into account, to judge actions in terms of *all* of their effects and not just a selection. Time and tradition may suggest that some factors are more important than others, but such decisions may be transitory and are subject to revision. The principal danger to avoid is a structure or procedure that opens the way to curing the disease by killing the patient.

Many of the normative variables currently in use in American society, and in other societies as well, are decidedly inadequate for contemporary needs. They derive mostly from traditional religion and moral discourse, with some additions from the law. Traditional ethics usually concentrated on development of broad principles that could be rigidly applied rather than on ways of justifying relative judgments based on comparisons. The principles of ethics were seldom stated in ways that provided an effective guide to action. The concepts found in ethics are therefore poorly adapted to comparing outcomes and developing rules of action that would actually enforce a specific choice in some situation. It is exceptionally difficult if not impossible, for example, to discuss the differences in quality of life between an educated, wealthy American and a poor, desperately deprived American using the language of moral philosophy. Differences in education and wealth convey information to those familiar with life in the various cultural strata defined by income, but the concepts needed to articulate those meanings and explore their relative significance have not yet been developed. This inadequacy creates some serious problems for disciplines, such as economics, that seek to fulfill the policymaker's needs. Choices are based on projected outcomes. Those projections are created using instruments produced within the empirical disciplines, hence are limited to the concepts employed in those instruments. But if the conceptual apparatus is normatively inadequate, the accuracy of the projections is actually irrelevant—the costs and benefits of action will not be adequately stated.

Two general points need to be made about the substance or content of any set of normative variables intended for use in policymaking. First, the variables will refer to the attributes of individual humans. Reasoned choice focuses on the impact of one person's actions on other persons, including the self. Man is the measure of things in any human priority system. The reason appears in a simple *reductio ad absurdum:* without human life, the choice enterprise as a whole is meaningless. There would be no one to make choices, no basis for choosing, and no one to care whether or not a choice was made. For human choosers, there is no alternative to what philosophers call radical individualism in ethics. Changes that cannot be attributed to human actors are not a suitable object for reasoned criticism; the critical apparatus deals with actions by humans and nothing else. Changes that do not affect any person, even if that is possible, would be normatively benign. Of course, a person who predicts or foresees a natural disaster and fails to warn a neighbor has used a natural event as an instrument of action and that action can be criticized. The natural disaster may elicit affective reaction but not reasoned criticism.

Radical individualism, which asserts that human actions are evaluated by reference to their human impact, is an essential assumption in any approach to reasoned action. It should not be confused with either methodological individualism, which claims that all explanations of human phenomena must be stated in terms of individual actions or intentions, or with "rugged individualism," which holds each individual solely responsible for his or her own welfare. Actions that alter social features are of uncertain significance until they have been extended to show their effects on particular persons. Choices are criticized by reference to the elements or members of society and not its features. An analogy to watches is mistaken; there is no external purpose to serve as a measure.

The major corollary to radical individualism, and the other prime assumption in the normative enterprise, is that one human life is the equal of any other, at least in the limited sense of life *qua* life. Operationally, if a choice must be made between two lives, and nothing is known beyond the humanity of those involved, there can be no reasoned grounds for choosing between them, no basis for preference that is not invidious and unacceptable. Of course, other information relating to age, health, behavior, and so on may allow differentiation that is defensible, but with respect to life alone, the choice cannot be made on any reasoned grounds. Assuming humanity as the basic measure, the individual as the unit of measurement, and the equality of one life with another does not solve the problems of reasoned choice. It does, however, influence the kinds of solutions that are considered acceptable, and would produce enormous changes in current practice if adopted and enforced. The assumptions may be thin but they are not trivial.

Without trying to specify the substance of the normative variables, some of their primary characteristics need to be identified. The variables are used to measure the condition or quality of individual human life. That life has both dimensionality and extension in time. Either or both aspects of life can be incorporated into the variables. Analytically, a full though not exhaustive description of any individual can be produced by specifying the observed values of some finite set of variables at a point in time. For the actions of one person to affect another, the value of at least one of those variables must be altered, or prevented from changing when it would otherwise change. Impact is measured in terms of the difference in the values of one or more variables in the set used to describe an individual or class at two points in time. The consequences of action, then, can be stated as one descriptive account of an individual or class *rather than* another different descriptive account of the same persons. There is no need to assess the normative quality of the situation described on an absolute scale. So long as a comparison of two or more states can generate reasons for preferring one to the others, that suffices for reasoned and corrigible choice. It is easy, for example, to find reasons for preferring a state of the individual in which the "malaria" variable is negative to a state in which it is positive. Generalized, the preference structure can be used to deal with that choice whenever it appears—it applies to the class of choices exemplified in the particular case.

Not all of the variables that can be used to describe individual humans have intrinsic normative significance. The normative implications of a given change in the value of some variable may not be determined directly; secondary and even tertiary effects may have to be examined. The structure of the normative variables must allow such complex assessments. How that is managed is best demonstrated by tracing the evolution of the structure. The root meaning of each normative variable, the quality being measured or compared, refers to some aspect of the condition of life of a human individual. The goal is a structure that allows the critic to judge whether the quality of life is being maintained or improved.

Development of a normative variable begins with some set of variables used to describe an individual at a point in time. Symbolizing each *variable* as (V), the selection can be enclosed in square brackets [  ] to show that the set is "open," that is, cannot be calculated. It signifies a selection and not a set of variables whose values are linked by rule. A description of the person is made by specifying the observed values of the selection of variables; the structure is unavoidably incomplete and could be extended indefinitely:

$$[ \ V_1 \ V_2 \ V_3 \ V_4 \ V_5 \ V_6 \ . \ . \ . V_n \ ]$$

To have an impact or effect on the individual that can be evaluated or criticized, human action must produce a change in the value of at least one of the variables within the set—or add a new variable to the collection, that is, change the value from zero to some positive integer.

Some attributes of the individual can be altered directly by another person, or by the self, producing an observable effect. Those attributes will be called *indicators* and symbolized as (VI). They do not measure the quality of human life directly, but are used in indirect measurement. The amount of physical damage inflicted upon the human body does not indicate the overall damage to the human life, for example. A small amount of damage to the eye may have a prolonged and enormous effect on life as a whole;

severe physical damage may have few if any lasting effects. The "life" that is used to judge such matters is a complex affair, of course, and has both duration and intensity. The indicators serve to connect that life to the external world, linking it to the actions of others. Structurally, they can be separated from the other attributes of the individual to form a special subset in the following manner:

$$[ \quad [VI_1 \ VI_2 \ \ldots \ VI_n \ ] \qquad [V_1 \ V_2 \ V_3 \ V_4 \ \ldots \ V_n \ ] \quad ]$$

The immediate or proximate effect of action is a change in the value of one of the indicator variables, VI. The impact of that change on the whole life, however, cannot be inferred from the indicator variables alone.

To assess the normative effects of a change in the indicator variables requires reference to a second set of individual attributes, the physical, cultural, intellectual, economic, and other characteristics of the person that mediate the impact of changes in the values of the indicator variables. Wealth cushions the effects of financial loss, physical condition the effects of illness, and so on. Such mediating factors will be called *buffer variables* (VB) and they are also viewed as a subset in the overall structure of individual attributes. The result looks like this:

$$[ \quad [VI_1 \ VI_2 \ \ldots \ VI_n \ ] \ [ \ VB_1 \ VB_2 \ \ldots \ VB_n \ ] \ [ \ V_1 \ V_2 \ V_3 \ \ldots \ V_n ] \quad ]$$

The buffer variables identify the classes of persons who are affected normatively in the same way by a common action. If a specific change is induced in the indicator variables, all those who share the same set of buffer variables will be influenced identically, however the calculations of effect are made. Put another way, the normative impact of action is measured by a combination of indicator and buffer variables; neither is sufficient taken alone. This point is of the greatest importance in policymaking. For example, the effect of a fixed weekly payment to poor persons will be the same only for those who share a common set of buffer variables. Determining that subset of the overall population might be extremely difficult. The complexity of the problem increases further because

any number of human attributes might serve as buffers for particular actions, producing differentiated effects within relatively
homogeneous populations.

The object to be captured by the normative variables, taken as
a whole, is the dimensions of life that are intrinsically significant,
valued for themselves and not for what they can bring about. They
will include such factors as continued existence, various psychic
states, health, freedom of action, access to culture, and so on.
The value of such variables is a very complex function, which must
be embodied in rules (R) linking the changes induced in the indicator
variables, the values taken by the buffer variables, and the concept
contained in the normative variable. To illustrate with a simple
case, the impact on individual life of a small monetary loss is not a
simple function of the amount lost. Impact depends on such other
factors as wealth, income, borrowing capacity, and, of course,
the dimensions of life used as a final measure. A small loss might
seriously impede individual development under some set of circumstances yet cause no serious effects for the same person at another
point in life. Rules (R) are therefore required that can combine
changes in the values of indicators with the values of appropriate
buffers to produce an overall value for the normative variable.
Such calculable structures are enclosed in parentheses (  ). The rules
are likely to be crude and approximate, of course, but that is often
all that decision requires.

Expressed pictorially, the resulting structure of choice looks
rather complex and forbidding, though its elements are relatively
commonplace:

$$[( [VI_1 \ VI_2 \ \ldots \ VI_n] \ [VB_1 \ VB_2 \ \ldots \ VB_n] \ [R_1 \ R_2 \ \ldots \ R_n ]) \ [V_1 \ V_2 \ V_3 \ \ldots \ V_n] \ ]$$

Actually, the structure serves to demonstrate the enormous capacity of the human nervous system, for it is used almost casually in
everyday life, as careful analysis of a real case will show very quickly.
Common usage has not produced a clear articulation of the structures and processes involved, but applications are well understood
and readily performed. The family that sits down to work out next
month's budget, calculating the effects of a variety of particular
expenditures or delays in spending on individual family members,

uses the same complex apparatus. When the individuals affected are familiar, and the actions and their consequences are well known, the complexities are easily managed—and there is often significant improvement in performance over time.

The substance of the normative variables cannot be identified using general concepts and the effects of action cannot be assessed in abstract or hypothetical terms. The range of possibilities is too great for useful speculation. Happily, reasoned choice is not frustrated by the absence of a complete set of normative variables. Any selection, however inadequate, can serve as a point of departure for real world choices. The diagram in figure 1 shows how the outcomes available for choice are generated and structured. For clarity, only two options (A and B) are assumed, but the principle is the same however large the range of possibilities to be explored. The illustration shows the effects of choice for just one class of persons. A separate structure would be required for each class in a real case. A probability estimate should be attached to the projections (1, 2, W, X, and so on) suggesting the reliability of the theory employed, the likelihood that the outcome will actually occur. At the boundaries of the structure there are sets of possible or suspected relations, shown with dotted lines. For example, reliable authorities may accept a relationship without having conclusive evidence for it—the relationship between cigarette smoking and lung cancer had that status for some time.

Having projected the outcomes to the limits of current knowledge, the values and probabilities developed for each normative variable are brought together into a matrix (see figure 2). Again, a separate structure is needed for each class of persons affected by choice. In complex situations, the result will be a three-dimensional lattice rather than a simple plane figure. The priority system created to solve the choice is developed from a comparison of outcomes structured in this way.

The process used to identify the preferred outcome in a set will usually involve complex weighing and balancing, for few actions produce positive benefits and no unwanted costs. Various strategies are used to reduce the number of options to manageable proportions—any option that contains positive values for certain variables may be excluded, for example. When dealing with the contribution that empirical disciplines such as economics can make to

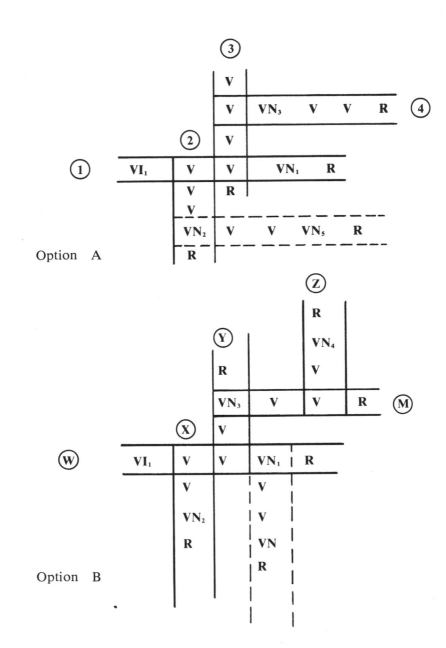

Option A

Option B

**Figure 1**

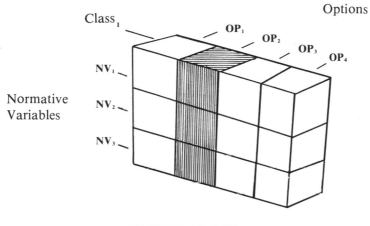

SINGLE CLASS

MULTI-CLASS

**Figure 2**

policymaking, these aspects of choice need not be examined in any detail. But it is obvious that much empirical study is needed to determine the priorities actually being used at present and to begin linking them systematically to particular consequences for specific classes of persons. Until such empirical studies have been completed, systematic efforts to improve current practice are unlikely to succeed.

PRIORITY SYSTEMS

Analytically, the instruments needed to make reasoned choices are created after the outcomes available have been structured to show their normative content and reasons have been found for preferring one outcome to the others. Historically, a clearly defined sequence is unlikely because of the priorities already in use and the common practice of acting or choosing out of habit or custom without any conscious effort to weigh costs and benefits. The substance of priorities cannot be established outside the context of particular choices, but it is worth noting that current practice will tend to continue, particularly in the short run. The normative variables and priorities in use will usually remain in use, whether or not they are adequate; they are very hard to replace, or even modify significantly, in a short time. That characteristic of ongoing social practice underscores the need for a careful examination of current usage. The kind of careful structuring of alternatives that is a necessary preliminary to reasoned choice seems to occur only rarely, whether in collective or individual actions. And systematic criticism of the inherited normative apparatus is even less common.

Assume that the two outcomes from which a choice must be made have been projected on the future in an adequate manner. Assume further that reasons have been found for preferring one outcome to the other. The instruments needed to make the choice must now be created. The reasons for preferring one outcome to the other provide the justification for accepting and using the instruments. Actions based on those instruments serve initially as a test of the instruments and ultimately as a test of the reasons offered for the preference.

Although it may not be obvious, *two* instruments are needed for reasoned choice. The first is a preference or priority system that can order the two outcomes; the second is a rule of action that will produce the preferred outcome in that situation. To take an example from medicine, the priority system would express a preference for life without malaria to life with malaria; the action rules would contain the prescribed mode of treatment expected to produce the preferred outcome. The priority structure is justified by the reasoning used to support a preference for one outcome rather than the other. The rules of action are justified by reference to the priority structure; application of the rules should produce the preferred outcome. However, the rules of action are derived from the theoretical apparatus used to project the available outcomes and not from the priority system. The two are logically and empirically independent. Both priorities and rules of action are stated in generalized form, obviously, and each is tested in use in the same way as any other instrument.

When the goal is reasoned choice based on the consequences of action, priority systems are built from below, beginning with the particular case and proceeding inductively, as in scientific theorizing. The priorities in use, however, have usually developed as general principles following the pattern established in classic moral philosophy. Philosophers have usually sought for universal principles of action rather than limited solutions for particular cases; the goal has been a generalized justification of principles based on absolute criteria rather than relative standards based on comparisons. Only rarely have moral philosophers concerned themselves with the consequences of accepting and applying their principles. Justification for ethical principles has been sought outside their consequences, and that has led to some very peculiar conceptions of both the nature of ethical decisions and the kind of reasoning required to justify them. Perhaps the most influential volume in ethics in the first half of the twentieth century, for example, argued that things or situations were chosen or evaluated by reference to a simple unanalyzable characteristic that was intrinsic to the thing evaluated, and no evidence could be produced to show the presence of the intrinsic quality.[4] The most influential volume thus far produced in the second half of the century, while it did not reject the possibility of producing evidence and supporting argument, asserted that the author's two fundamental principles should be accepted because rational men placed in a peculiar and imaginary situation called the "original position" would choose those two principles in preference to any available alternatives.[5] Despite the curious nature of such arguments, they are taken very seriously indeed within philosophy.

Even if the inadequacy of justification is ignored, many of the principles that philosophers recommend turn out to be vacuous, have no implications for action and hence cannot serve as a guide to action. The most famous of them is probably Immanuel Kant's "categorical imperative," which urged individuals to act in such manner that the principle underlying their actions could be universalized: That is tantamount to telling an angler not to remove from the lake any fish whose absence would disturb the ecological balance in a negative way. The rule may sound reasonable but it cannot be applied; the result is a special kind of question begging all too common in moral philosophy. Despite its inadequacies, faith in the postulational and universalized approach to normative questions persists. Moreover, it is usually coupled with a search for an integrated, overarching structure able to handle *all* normative problems and not for piecemeal solutions to particular problems. A parallel error is committed by the "grand theorists" of sociology, notably Talcott Parsons.[6] Much of economic theory has developed in the same tradition.

Yet the requirements of reasoned choice clearly indicate the need to proceed in the opposite direction, beginning with the particular case. The overall ethic need not be a single integrated structure; indeed, that is very unlikely even in the distant future, and probably undesirable since it would indicate moral fossilization. Each segment of an ethic, like each linked pair of variables in theory, can have an independent existence, fully legitimized and justified. The overall structure must be ordered transitively, of course; preference patterns in one subset must be consonant with preference patterns in the others. That is, if A is preferred to B in one place it must be preferred to B in the others. However, the same ordering is not required in compound structures. Preferring A to B does not entail preferring (A + X) to (B + X), as preferring tea to coffee does not require preferring tea with cream to coffee with cream. That characteristic of ordered priorities supplies the escape clause that makes compromise feasible and constructive.

## POLICIES

A priority system, produced by generalizing the solution to a particular choice problem, informs the user what to prefer but provides no guidance about how to achieve it. The priority system must be *applied* to the particular case; the preferred outcome must somehow be brought about. Another instrument is required for that purpose. It will contain a rule of action or guide to action; such rules of action are here labeled *policies*. In medicine, for example, a common priority is "good" health, invariably preferred to its antonym, "poor" health. Applying that priority to a person suffering from malaria clearly entails elimination of the disease. The preference is readily established and easily justified. All that remains is to specify the course of treatment that will actually produce the preferred outcome. That course of treatment, consisting of interrelated sets of rules of action, corresponds precisely to the meaning of policy adopted here. Obviously, a policy will incorporate a theory, and it will be closely linked to the theories used to project the set of options from which choice is made. The theory is constrained, however, by the need to produce the preferred outcome and still maintain the structured set of costs and benefits that was used to determine the preference.

To pursue the illustration, there are some situations in which the available supply of theories indicates that malaria does not figure into the outcomes possible for the individual—visitors to the Arctic regions usually need not be concerned with the disease. But the tourist in certain areas of Africa or Central America who accepts a priority system in which no malaria is preferred to malaria must include that possibility in the available options. How to achieve or maintain the preferred condition? The particular situation in which the preference system originated may not be parallel, hence simple extrapolation is not an adequate procedure in all cases. The search for policy must return to the basic theory used to project the outcomes on which the preference is based. The theory will include some statement about either the causes of the disease or the means by which it can be prevented or eliminated; otherwise, no projection of consequences could be made. If theory asserts that malaria is transmitted by mosquito bite, various lines of action are open to the individual. Any technique that avoids contact with mosquitos is acceptable; each will have its own sets of costs and benefits. The person may move to an area in which there are no mosquitos; the mosquito can be attacked and killed, with varying degrees of efficiency. Any line of action can serve as an acceptable policy if it leads to the preferred outcome and does not alter the original cost-benefit balance. Applying the policy may lead to a reexamination of preferences—if unanticipated costs appear, for example—but the basic structures and processes will remain the same. Note that a policy serves to integrate empirical and normative knowledge through use in a unique manner. Policies are tested against both the priority system and accepted theory. Acting on a policy serves to test the priority because it produces the preferred situation; it also tests the underlying theory, again by reference to the alternative produced. For the policy to be acceptable, both dimensions must survive the test.

Summarizing briefly, within the theory of knowledge, a set of rules that specify the means used to produce the preferred outcome from among a given set of options is required for action. Such rules are here labeled *policies*. Contextually, a policy is a set of rules of action that serve to apply a priority system to a particular situation. To *apply* means simply to act as the structure demands or requires. The rules must be fully adequate, for criticism and testing do not permit interpretation of meaning. If the rules do not *force* the action there is no test of the rules. Policies are criticized in both empirical and normative terms, comparing results obtained with predictions generated within the theory and with the outcome preferred under the accepted priority system. However labeled, instruments that can perform these functions are necessary for reasoned and corrigible action. Such guides to action link the empirical and normative structures available to real world human actors. So construed, policies are essential for maintaining and improving the human situation, and they can be created and improved within the limits of human capacity. The definition fulfills the conditions of adequacy established for policies at the outset of the inquiry. Further, it corresponds reasonably well with contemporary usage in academic and governmental circles, though the meaning here tends to be much more precise and the requirements are more rigorously stated. In real world policymaking or policy analysis, those requirements are seldom satisfied; most of the "policies" developed in individual and collective affairs acquire status by attribution rather than by systematic development, justification, and testing.

A fairly dramatic illustration of the difference between ordinary usage and the precise technical definition generated within the theory of knowledge emerges if current practices within government are transferred to the field of medicine. In medicine, the prescribed treatment for illness is precisely analogous to the meaning of policy accepted here. Medical policies are action rules that serve a normative purpose, though the purpose tends to be suppressed or assumed. The rules develop as solutions to particular cases, are generalized to fit classes of cases, and are subjected to more or less continuous testing in use, which leads to increasing precision in statements of limiting conditions. Evaluation of medical policies takes into account *all* of the normatively relevant effects of particular modes of treatment, to the extent they can be identified. In short, a medical policy summarizes the experience gained from the interaction of priorities and theories, tested in a specific case.

Suppose that the conception of policy and policymaking found in such areas of governmental action as public housing were transferred to the field of medicine. The ensuing changes would be startling, not to say alarming. No effort would be made to ascertain the medical needs of individual patients. Instead, a selection of symptoms, some irrelevant and some inadequate for particular diseases, would be aggregated, national averages would be computed, and treatment prescribed for the average case. The cost of treatment would be limited in advance to an amount determined by projecting average costs for previous years. So far as possible, the consequences of treatment for the individual patient would be ignored. If public outcry, or soaring costs, forced attention to consequences, only effects favorable to the policy would be reported. In due course, the prescribed treatment would be replaced or abandoned, even though the records showed that the treatment worked well for certain kinds of illness. Discussion and criticism, within government and in academia, would focus on major failures, ignoring success. In most cases, the patient would be blamed for failures and the validity of the treatment would be maintained disregarding evidence. What is distressing is the extent to which this functional account, though exaggerated for dramatic emphasis, is fundamentally accurate.[7]

SOME COMPLICATIONS

A number of additional requirements must be met before policies can be made defensible and corrigible. Some are not obvious, particularly in the case of collective actions, and need explicit statement. Most are stringent and difficult to apply in everyday affairs. But the requirements are a function of purposes sought and limiting conditions imposed by nature. Although it may be necessary to reserve them for major occasions, like Sunday-best clothing, the conditions must be met if policies are to serve significant human purposes yet remain defensible and corrigible. To refuse the limits because they are difficult to satisfy is like searching for lost keys in a lighted area because visibility is poor at the place where the keys were lost.

The requirements for reasoned policy tend to be severe, but there is no need to seek out complex and sophisticated issues, or large and powerful collective actors, to study the process. All of the essentials occur in simple, everyday cases. In fact, the requirements and hazards are best demonstrated using such illustrations. The football coach who teaches his players how to block an opponent effectively has provided them with a reasoned policy for dealing with a range of specific situations that recur regularly in each game. The retail store that refunds the purchase price on undamaged goods returned within a specified number of days after purchase has developed an equivalent instrument. Even the individual who makes it a rule not to drive an automobile after consuming more than two strong alcoholic drinks has developed or borrowed a sound, reasoned policy. The necessary conditions for success are the same for everyone, whether individual or collectivity, powerful or weak, sophisticated or naive. The conditions are more difficult to satisfy in collective actions, for reasons to be explored below, but there are no differences in principle. It is often said, "There is no such thing as Chinese physics," meaning that the rules are the same for everyone. Precisely the same condition obtains in policymaking.

Returning to complications and subtleties, one of the more misleading characteristics of contemporary usage is the common practice of stating policies in the injunctive form: take two aspirins each hour, stop at all intersections, avoid mosquitos of any kind, and so on. Unless policies force specific actions in appropriate situations, they are untestable, for the inferential chain linking action to consequence would be broken. An action that is consistent with a policy is not necessarily an application. The action must be formally entailed once the policy is accepted. The injunctive form serves to reinforce that requirement, and to that extent is justified. But policies are not wholly independent instruments; they are one element in a complex solution to a choice problem. The contingent relations between policy, priority system, and the theories used to project outcomes has one very important implication for policymaker and critic. The analytic separation of policy and priority must be maintained rigorously. Policies are generalized rules of action; priorities are generalized preferences. If the two are collapsed and the injunctive form is retained as a way of forcing specific actions, the substance of the collapsed rule will be a preference and not an action rule. In effect, collapsing the two structures substitutes an ethic of rules for an ethic of consequences. To return to an earlier example, the injunction, Do not remove fish from this lake if that action will disturb the ecological balance, actually requires the actor or critic to generate a preference ordering of the available options, to decide whether or not the ecological balance will be worsened in a particular case. To make that decision, a priority system must be created to fit the case and reasons sought for assuming that one is preferable to or worse than the other. But once that was done, there would be no reason to formulate the policy in the original form, and the original priority structure would be superseded. The rule of action would incorporate specific instructions for dealing with the limited class of cases exemplified by the fish actually caught. Collapsing the structure leads to a suppressed form of question begging; the question of priorities is circumvented yet the appearance of solution is maintained by using a Delphic pronouncement in injunctive form. The argument is somewhat tortuous but the principle involved is important enough to justify the time required to follow it to its conclusion.

The integration of empirical and normative elements in a single policy forces a test of the combined structure which poses some special difficulties for the critic. The consequences of applying a policy actually test an empirical-normative combination. Assessing the effects may lead to changes in priority system, in policy, in both, or in neither, depending on the situation. To illustrate, consider a choice among coins guided by a priority system in which more monetary value is preferred to less, other things equal. A rule such as "Choose the largest coin" may seem an adequate policy for producing the preferred outcome (greater monetary value). Offered a choice from a selection of coins, that policy may in fact operate successfully a number of times. But in any situation where choice lies between a small valuable coin and a large coin worth very little, the policy, correctly applied, will produce results that conflict with the priority system. If the priority system is examined and retained (by reference to experience) then the policy will have to be changed.

Complex rules can be developed for calculating the monetary value of a variety of coins and incorporated into the accepted policy—as in a coin dealer's operations. Suppose, however, that a choice is offered between coins of approximately equal value, but the monetary value of one coin is very slightly greater than the others and the sentimental value of a different coin is significantly greater than the sentimental value of any of the others. Applying the established policy will produce results that satisfy the original priority system but will not be sustained by examination of the adequacy of that priority. In this case, the normative structure can be modified by adding another variable (sentimental value of the coin) to the set used to describe the content of the available outcomes. A fairly complex rule would then have to be developed for comparing the importance of sentiment and monetary value—in effect, yet another variable would have to be produced that could be used to make the needed comparisons. That additional variable presumably could be found within the set used to identify the dimensions of life accorded intrinsic significance when the ethic was developed.

A slightly different series of problems arises from the special role played by the individual case in making and testing policy. Here, the field of medicine offers the clearest examples available. The tools needed for making reasoned choices are always developed out of the individual case and tested against other individual cases. The physician deals almost entirely with a *case* of measles and not with measles in the aggregate, unless an article about measles is being prepared for a journal. It follows that the case study plays a basic role in all forms of policymaking, as in medicine. Cases may be aggregated, of course, but *after* study and not to facilitate study. Aggregates cannot be used to develop treatments. These considerations suggest a need for a major reorientation of systematic inquiry when the purpose is to contribute to reasoned policymaking. In general, a policy that is made without reference to a specific case is a policy without applications. A policy is a solution to a particular case that has been generalized; generalization is subsequent to solution. A policy that solves one case automatically solves the class of cases that one case defines. If the class is significant, the policy is worth having. The procedure cannot be reversed. The class cannot be defined prior to the solution of the particular case without risking heterogeneity within the class that would frustrate efforts to apply the policy successfully. There is a major difference between postulating a general principle without reference to particulars and then deriving specific instances from it and generalizing established relations and testing the result. The former is mere postulation; the latter is the essence of the inductive procedure that is the hallmark of modern science. Economists rely very heavily on postulation, as will be apparent in chapter 5. That creates some major difficulties for policymakers seeking to use economics in their work.

A related error, equally common, is to treat ideals or aspirations as policies, or as priorities from which policies can be derived. Ideals by definition are beyond human capacity, unreachable states accessible only in imagination. Such purposes cannot be part of a reasoned choice structure. There is no way to determine whether or not a particular action is a move toward an ideal or away from it until the route to the goal has been charted completely. When that occurs, however, the ideal is no longer an ideal but an attainable option. Ideals are technically inadequate, given the requirements for reasoned action so long as they remain ideals. Further, the use of ideals as points of reference for choice fosters static perfectionism in normative matters to the extent that change is equated with deterioration or retrogression. The pragmatic-instrumentalist conception of reasoned policies as instruments that can be created by humans for improving the human situation within the limits of human capacity accords far better with past human performance—and detracts less from human stature.

Some of the minor implications of accepting the conception of policy developed within the theory of knowledge need be noted briefly. For one thing, the focus on curing, on improving existing conditions, eliminates the unfortunate tendency within academia to begin inquiry with the pursuit of origins. Whether the practice originated with Darwin, or reflects an earlier tradition, the result is gross inefficiency if the purpose of inquiry is to assist the policymaker. There is no need to know the origin of every human situation in order to improve it, just as the physician need not know the cause of a disease to effect a cure or develop a treatment—diabetes, whose cause is unknown but whose treatment is well established, provides the perfect illustration. When the cause of an event is known, it may facilitate more effective or efficient control over events, but knowledge of causes is prerequisite to controlling events only for a limited class of cases. In policymaking, the central concern is to control future events and not to understand the past. Primary emphasis should be placed on the search for cures and not causes. As a corollary, successes are more likely to suggest sound policies than are failures. To a surprising degree, social science has focused on breakdown and failure, the addict and not the person who has overcome the habit, for example, or the minority group and not those who treat minorities in a prejudicial manner. Concentrating on the search for cures should help to remedy the imbalance; certainly it is unlikely that an inquiry directed toward a cure for prejudicial behavior would focus on the minority that suffers from the practice. Finally, a strategy oriented to curing should help turn attention to the need for prevention. To take a common example, it is well known that if humans could be led to adopt a few simple rules of conduct—eat properly, rest adequately, and get enough exercise—that would do more to improve health within the society than all the medical research that contemporary resources could purchase. Similar opportunities for preventive action need to be located and exploited through reasoned policymaking, particularly in collective affairs.

In the recommended conception of policymaking, statements of policy are treated as simple actions that have their own unique consequences rather than genuine policies. Much needless confusion is thereby eliminated. And the practice ensures that the costs and benefits of policy announcements are included within the costs and benefits of the policy. Such considerations are not new, of course, but the fact that the approach to policy adopted here demands them is another sound reason for taking it seriously.

Finally, it should be fairly obvious that the major substantive areas of collective action cannot possibly be controlled by a single rule or set of rules. Terms such as "foreign policy" or "housing policy" are at best only labels for mixed aggregates of rules. Unfortunately, common usage and contemporary governmental practice tend to ignore impossibility; efforts to create, apply, and criticize such global policies are taken very seriously. Analytically, the structures are no more than gigantic division fallacies. A national housing policy is improved by altering its constituent elements; they may range from interest rates and construction standards through statements of eligibility for benefits and management procedures. Each of these areas is criticized by reference to the still more specific effects produced by even narrower rules of action. The principle involved is most clearly illustrated by efforts to deal with automobile accidents. Until that statistical aggregate has been broken down to show causal relations, reasoned policy expected to reduce automobile accidents is beyond reach. Only such drastic actions as removing all automobiles from the highway can actually be developed out of consideration of the aggregate as a whole. Even reducing the national speed limit requires an assumption about the relation between accidents and speed. And disaggregation of the statistics is not automatic. If the aggregate cannot be analyzed, remedial action on reasoned grounds may be effectively ruled out. The key is the way in which the aggregate is constructed. If a unidirectional conceptual transformation is carried out in the aggregation process, disaggregation will cease at that point, and policy must be made at that point, or deferred.

POLICYMAKING

Reasoned policymaking emerges from the analysis of choice as a complex, difficult, and problematic human activity. That will not surprise those who have tried to manage individual or collective affairs systematically and develop the apparatus needed to improve performance.[8] Policymaking can be characterized in various ways, each illustrating a different aspect of the process and of the problems associated with it. Here, the principal concern is with social policy, since that is the area in which the use of economics is most critical. But the principles involved are much the same, whether the policy is meant to guide individual action, collective action, or private business. Special emphasis is placed on kinds of changes required to place social policy on a sound intellectual base, to render it justifiable and corrigible, because that is the most urgent need at the present time.

Policymaking is the application of human knowledge and resources to the conduct of human affairs. The purpose of the enterprise is to develop rules of action that will apply established priorities to specific situations and by doing so maintain or improve the quality of life of the human population affected. The prime constraint on the policymaker is the available supply of knowledge and resources and efforts to increase the supply of knowledge available are powerfully justified if that knowledge is required for policymaking. That is perhaps the sense in which the demand for "relevance" is most readily justified within academic life. Policymaking can also be construed as a special kind of engineering, a reasoned effort to improve the human situation. However, the pejorative overtones usually attached to the term "social engineering" must be foregone. There is no reason why systematic policymaking cannot lead to a hands-off policy as well as to active intervention. The target population may include all members of a large society or only a single person (the policymaker); reasoned policymaking can serve individual interests as well as the collective interest. The critical procedures are identical, whatever the size of the population affected.

The specific factors weighed in reasoned choice will vary with actor, situation, resources, and a host of other considerations. The knowledge requirements, however, will take the same general form whatever the details of circumstance. Almost any contribution to knowledge can find a use somewhere in the policymaking process, as will be made clear in chapter 4. Predictions can be used to locate areas in society that require future action—projected fuel or water shortages, for example. Theories of a particular kind are needed for projecting the outcomes from which choices are made and for developing the policies used to achieve the preferred outcome. Priority systems must be available for ordering the outcomes; they are absolutely contingent upon an adequate set of normative variables. And behind the intellectual instruments used directly in policymaking there is a need for adequate and accurate descriptions, for logical capacity, for a sound language, for institutional arrangements able to generate and use information, and so on.

At yet another level, policymaking is constrained by the availability of resources and technology, the boundaries established for the authority of the policymaker, the information available about the conditions of life of the target population, the kind of decisionmaking machinery employed in society, the normative commitments of those whose assent is required to put policy in force, and so on. In addition to creating and applying rules of action, the overall process of policymaking is quite properly taken to include development of an adequate monitoring or feedback system, able to measure the effects of action over time, using appropriate concepts. Those data must then be processed, their implications examined, and the resulting recommendations fed into the policymaking machinery in an effective way. To gather data and process it means nothing if there is no learning or the results are not used. Some or all of these activities lie outside the competence of any individual policymaker. The influence of the established social machinery is usually dominant. Efforts to produce reasoned and corrigible policies can be frustrated at countless points in the process, particularly as the enterprise is presently organized and carried out. Careful analysis of the necessary conditions for reasoned policymaking is therefore essential if there is to be any serious improvement.

Two of the changes in current practice needed to put policymaking on a sound basis stand out as particularly important. First, the effects of action should be weighed solely in terms of changes induced in the lives of particular persons. Thinking in these terms would literally revolutionize current practice, and not in the United States alone. European nations tend to have more information about their citizens than is available in the United States or Canada, but the change in emphasis would be very difficult to introduce and enforce on either continent. Second, some major changes would be needed in the institutional arrangements that have been established in all of the Western democracies before the necessary conditions for reasoned policymaking could be created. Again, there is little likelihood that such changes could be made in the short run, but the nature of the requirement, and the implications of the changes for the wider society, are worth exploration.

*Radical Individualism.* Reasoned policymaking intended to maintain or improve the human situation for an indentifiable population is unavoidably contingent upon acceptance of two normative assumptions. One is that the ultimate measure of value for humans is the individual human life; the other is that in the limited sense of life *qua* life, one life is the equal of any other. There is no acceptable set of alternative assumptions available. Enforcement of the two fundamentals would have enormous implications for nearly every society on earth. In due course, the implications of institutional change for particular populations might be well enough established to allow policymakers to focus on producing such changes; even then, the ultimate criterion would remain the effects of action on the individual.

At the very least, that commitment would show the extent to which current policies are made in near-total ignorance of the consequences of action, or without adequate consideration of the side-effects of action on secondary populations. In almost every discussion of the effects of public policy, the primary concern is a social institution or some generalized or aggregated feature of society such as national security or expenditure per person for particular services. The detailed effect of collective action on a specific target population is rarely examined. Indeed, it would be difficult to determine given present recordkeeping practices. The greater the stakes involved, the further removed from the individual are the concepts used to state outcomes or argue policies. Those who govern speak often of providing security, protecting vital interests, maintaining economic stability, or increasing well-being and prosperity and rarely if at all about effects on particular classes, suitably aggregated. The general public apparently agrees that such empty phrases can be translated into meaningful criteria for assessing the costs and benefits of choice. Yet even the most casual effort to make these assessments demonstrates the futility of the enterprise both quickly and decisively.

If the consequences of collective action are stated in terms of changes in various social features, their normative significance cannot be determined and improvement in performance is ruled out in principle. The necessary conditions for corrigibility have not been met. In the circumstances, the tendency for "policies" to become rhetorical conveniences, used and discarded like paper cups at a water fountain, is understandable if deplorable. There are few documented cases where collective policies have been improved over time. Existing institutional arrangements are such that changing current practice is likely to be very difficult. Even granting the will to change, and the needed resources, the information and knowledge required to produce improvements deliberately are in most cases beyond reach.

To illustrate, one of the preconditions to reasoned improvement in policymaking is the availability of enough baseline information to determine the effects of action. Without some inventory of the population, sufficiently rich and detailed to show the full range of effects flowing from policy, the minimum conditions for correcting and improving policy cannot be satisfied. Only rarely are large populations identically affected by a common external action; an atomic weapon is a great leveler in at least two senses, but it has few parallels. Furthermore, the population inventory cannot be limited to a specific target population but must include all persons affected by the policy, whether the effect is intended or not. The assumption, very common in discussions of foreign affairs, that the population of a large nation-state is affected homogeneously by the actions of other nations is obviously false. The impact of a military draft, for example, has varied enormously within the United States depending on race, income, education, and other characteristics of the population examined. Typologies of national populations that can show the impact of a range of public actions are not available. Even such vital matters as the amount of unemployment in society are crudely and inadequately monitored. Moreover, no one way of ordering large populations will be equally useful for all policymakers. The eye specialist and foot doctor may use some common information about patients, but each requires specialized data that would not be useful to the other and a single examination system meant to serve both might be quite wasteful. At present, neither the theoretical apparatus, the normative machinery, or the institutional arrangements required for developing an adequate population inventory is available.[9]

The importance of having no basic social inventory can hardly be exaggerated. At one level, reasoned policymaking is nothing more than inventory management of a particular kind. That is, the effects of action are identified precisely as differences in the defining characteristics of a target population at two points in time. If the initial condition of the population is unknown, the effects of action are unavoidably indeterminate. Inventories also serve as devices for locating subpopulations whose conditions of life diverge so profoundly from the rest of society that urgent collective action is required. They provide an essential baseline for structuring the jurisdiction of social agencies concerned with specific subpopulations. Finally, the content of the social inventory should serve as an indicator of the competence as well as the compassion of the society that produces it. Deplorable social practices, such as discriminating against internal minorities or discounting the effects of national policy beyond the national borders will usually be reflected in the inventory. More positively, because the social inventory can provide exemplification of the meaning of "fortunate" and "unfortunate" within the society at a point in time, it is an invaluable tool for those seeking justification for national priorities. Finally, a sound inventory supplies a base for calculating the costs of implementing different priorities and a needed check on the operation of existing institutions for making and improving policy.

The foregoing discussion deliberately ignores the obstacles to change that are usually entrenched in large and complex societies. In some parts of the world, the pressing need is to maintain present conditions, or even to avoid losing ground too rapidly in periods of stress; positive improvements may be out of the question. The capacity to make large-scale improvements in the conditions of life of very large populations has only recently been acquired. Only a few societies possess that capacity at present; none has developed its use very systematically. In most cases, technological improvements have contributed most to those already well off and not to those in severe distress. Here the experience that has been gained providing assistance to less-developed nations illustrates the process very well, reflecting the historical course of events within the developed nations themselves. Usually, the less fortunate have been provided with limited access to goods and services hitherto reserved for and valued by the better off. The appropriateness of the priorities applied, whether for developed or less-developed societies, usually has been ignored. Simple quantitative increases in some aggregate feature of society such as national income has been identified implicitly with qualitative improvements in the life of the individual. Yet as William C. Thiesenhusen points out, "The truth that groups of people are differentially (and some even adversely) affected by a rising national average income is hardly a revelation to those who care to recall their reading of Dickens."[10] The truth is amply documented, both in foreign assistance and within American society.

*Institutional Arrangements*    For any of the large representative democracies, major changes in existing institutional arrangements would be required before the necessary conditions for reasoned policymaking could be created. In the United States, three aspects of current practice would make the transition particularly difficult. First, there is no regular procedure for monitoring the initial choice among choices that society must take, no point where the gamut of collective actions is brought together and rationalized. Moreover, the absence of such institutional arrangements is considered a positive virtue and change would be strongly resisted. Second, the present decisionmaking machinery is used both to develop proposed policies and to adopt them authoritatively. Both decisions emerge from the interactions of the same set of interests. Third, the educational system does not produce the capacity for reasoned action or criticism that policymaking, or democratic citizenship, demands. Considered as knowledge consumers, most citizens are incompetent. Under these circumstances, the ordinary citizen must depend almost entirely on the competence and integrity of those who control the decisionmaking machinery. In effect, the incompetent knowledge consumer cannot participate meaningfully in society and the collectivity loses any benefits that might be gained by adding that individual's experience to the collective judgment.

In general, the large representative democracies are not organized to review options available to the whole society and allocate resources accordingly. Indeed, it is usually difficult to modify, eliminate, or even augment established operations except in dire emergencies. The best indicator of inadequacy of existing arrangements is found in the common practice of treating the national budget as the central focus for policy decisions. Strictly speaking, no budget of that size can function as a policy instrument; the effects of change are literally unforeseeable because of the way budgets are prepared and integrated. In the United States, as elsewhere, the major segments of the budget are treated as independent elements with unique histories. Resource allocations are decided by reference to prior allocations; assessment of need is virtually unknown, and would not be possible in most cases. Understandably, budget changes are hardly ever linked to comparative needs. Moreover, budgetary practice is not conceived in such terms. Budgeted amounts are raised or lowered independently within global limits; they are established mainly by reference to prior spending rather than needs. The practice of incrementalism alone suffices to rule out reasoned control of national resource allocation.[11]

Use of the same collective agency to structure the substance of policy and then adopt it authoritatively, strongly reinforces the bias against reasoned action built into contemporary social institutions. Such collective actions are decided by formal aggregation of individual decisions—in effect, out of the interaction of competing particular concerns. The link between individual action and its consequences and the collective decision and its consequences cannot be foreseen and the two may be quite incompatible. As a result, such collective decisionmaking agencies become a special class of natural phenomena, like floods or earthquakes. They are beyond reasoned criticism because capacity and responsibility cannot be fixed. Various solutions to a well-known problem have been proposed; none has been effective. An adequate theory of representation, if accepted by everyone involved, could integrate individual and collective choices. Others have suggested recourse to history and tradition, reliance upon a "general will," disciplined political parties, and parliamentary government, among others. Until some change is made, reasoned criticism of the decisions or actions of collective bodies such as Congress is effectively ruled out. There is no way to determine the alternatives, since those alternatives must be a real and practical possibility.

The likelihood that reasoned policies can be developed by collective decisioning units is significantly lessened if the government system is "reactive" rather than "directive." In a directive system, best exemplified by the Soviet Union or China, future planning is undertaken deliberately and the government seeks policies that will produce preferred future states in the society. Whether or not they succeed, the principle involved is well established. In a reactive system such as the United States, the government does very little to initiate policy and plan for the future. The government is not assigned primary responsibility for achieving desired future social states; indeed, its ability to perform that function is likely to be questioned. Instead, such political systems react to internal and external pressures, generating "policies" that are responses rather than positive efforts. The frustrations encountered by reactive systems in foreign affairs are often noted; the implications for domestic affairs tend to be ignored or overlooked. Obviously, a reactive system, with its accompanying institutions and norms, will find it difficult to create and improve reasoned policies. In fact, serious efforts to generate policies aimed at future improvements could be regarded as conflicting with the nation's fundamental priorities and institutional arrangements.

The outlook for reasoned policymaking darkens still more if the society relies excessively on compromise to handle internal conflict. No society can function effectively without compromise, of course; it avoids the disruption that comes with open conflict. But no society can compromise endlessly without serious debilitation of the institutional arrangements that order social affairs. The reason is found in the nature of compromise, for the procedure works by *evading* conflicts in priorities. If Jones prefers A to B and Smith prefers B to A, and neither will yield, an impasse has been reached. If each has a private army, the effect could be disastrous. Compromise serves to change the content of the choice, evading the impasse. If some (X) can be found that allows both Smith and Jones to prefer (A + X) to (B + X), the dilemma is resolved. Not infrequently, X is located in the public treasury. The resemblance to blackmail is not coincidence. When continued disagreement is likely to produce serious disruption and vast social costs, compromise may be essential. But if every disagreement is compromised, as tends to happen in reactive systems, improvement in priorities is ruled out. The long-run effect of static priorities or values is likely to be even more disastrous than continued disagreement over priorities, particularly in periods of rapid social change.

Some of the conceptual confusion associated with the use of collective decisionmaking units has been masked by the practice of personalizing the actions of collectivities. "The United States Senate today went on record . . ." or "The British Cabinet decided today . . ." are statements that exemplify the process. Corporations, Congress, and courts are not human, Marx and the Supreme Court notwithstanding. Organizations may be legal persons but they are only useful fictions. It is sometimes very expedient to be able to construe an organization as an actor, but that practice tends to inhibit close scrutiny of what may well be the most important form of uncontrolled consequentiality at large in the world at the present time.

The massive failure of education in the large Western democracies provides the third major impediment to development of reasoned policymaking. The effect of the failure is felt in two ways: the needed capacity is not generated among policymakers; the general public lacks the critical ability required to generate support for improvements. In recent years, the available supply of natural talent, of persons able to learn how to learn from experience without external assistance, has been diluted more and more as society's need for intellectual skill has increased. The trend is most readily seen in the less-developed nations but no less significant in the advanced industrial nations. Assessments of the degree of inadequacy may vary but there is little disagreement on the fundamental point.

Socially, some of the effects of the educational breakdown have been obscured by technological advances and the increasing number of "prepackaged" arrangements they have made possible. Organizations have been created that provide individuals, at cost, a range of substitutes for intellectual skills not developed in the schools. The technique serves to extend the usefulness of the highly skilled very substantially. But increased urbanization and dependence, coupled with an enormous decrease in individual opportunities to acquire intellectual skills by "tinkering" or trial and error methods, has greatly increased the pressure on the schools. If the classroom is not structured to provide an environment in which youth can learn how to learn, such competence is unlikely to be acquired. No other agency within the society has the same potential for generating the needed skills. But there are few indications that those who operate the schools know the kinds of skills required or how they might be improved. Indeed, it seems likely that the schools would strongly oppose efforts to induce improved critical performance, for that would certainly entail imposition of performance criteria on administrators and faculty as well as students.

Finally, the trend to increased centralization in decisionmaking, in both public and private affairs, has tended to mask the growing need for greater individual capacity in intellectual matters. The realization that society's problems cannot be resolved by a small handful of central planners and policymakers is emerging slowly and painfully, and is not yet influential. As the scale of social organization increases, the potential for central planning decreases steadily, even with all of the advantages provided by computerized equipment. In complex organizations, if reasoned and corrigible policies are the goal, planning and policymaking are necessarily functions of the periphery and not the center. The center is well situated for rationalizing competing demands on resources, or for mobilizing resources equitably, but not for disposing them effectively and humanely.

The reasoning is inescapable. A corrigible policy must be made at the point in an organization where the consequences of action can be calculated accurately. The information required for making such policies cannot be transported to a central planner without elision and condensation. Much of what is known locally cannot be articulated and sent; what is forwarded to the center is a selection, and a compression, of what is known. Budgets provide a good illustration of the weakness of the process. The various components are aggregated from below but once this is done they cannot be disaggregated to restore the original meaning. The best hope for large-scale policymaking is to create an overall structure and a climate of trust and mutual respect in which local policymaking can take place. Scale forces decentralization; decentralization increases the need for local competence in policymaking and administration. That is the relatively simple lesson that society has been slow to learn in this century. As the Western democracies are gradually converted from reactive to directive systems, and the pace of conversion seems to be accelerating, the urgency of the problem will surely increase and the costs of inadequate education can be expected to rise astronomically.

## NOTES

1. See John Hospers, *Human Conduct: An Introduction to the Problems of Ethics* (Harcourt, Brace and World, 1961). For comparison, see C. D. Broad, *Five Types of Ethical Theory* (Littlefield, Adams, 1959); John Dewey, *The Public and its Problems* (Henry Holt, 1927); idem, *Theory of the Moral Life* (Holt, Rinehart and Winston, 1960); William K. Frankena, *Ethics* (Prentice-Hall, 1963); D. M. Mackinnon, *A Study in Ethical Theory* (Collier Books, 1962); Nicholas Rescher, ed., *The Logic of Decision and Action* (University of Pittsburgh Press, n.d.); Milton Rokeach, *The Nature of Human Values* (Free Press, 1973); Stephen Toulmin, *The Place of Reason in Ethics* (Cambridge University Press, 1960); Mary Warnock, *Ethics Since 1900,* 2d ed. (Oxford University Press, 1966).

2. Some classic statements of this problem were made by Rousseau and Edmund Burke, but see Kenneth J. Arrow, *Social Choice and Individual Values,* 2d ed. (Yale University Press, 1963); James M. Buchanan and Gordon Tullock, *The Calculus of Consent: Logical Foundations of Constitutional Democracy* (University of Michigan Press, 1962); Guido Calabresi and Philip Bobbitt, *Tragic Choices* (W. W. Norton, 1978); Dennis C. Mueller, *Public Choice* (Cambridge University Press, 1979); Mancur Olson, *The Logic of Collective Action: Public Goods and the Theory of Groups* (Harvard University Press, 1965); William H. Riker, *The Theory of Political Coalitions* (Yale University Press, 1962).

3. For an interesting application of this idea in economics, see Victor Zarnowitz, "On the Accuracy and Properties of Recent Macroeconomic

Forecasts," *American Economic Review* 68 (May 1978): 313-19, where it is shown that the quality of economic forecasts drops very sharply after a period of two to four quarters.

4. George Edward Moore, *Principia Ethica* (Cambridge University Press, 1960), especially ch. 1.

5. John Rawls, *A Theory of Justice* (Harvard University Press, 1971), especially ch. 3.

6. See Eugene J. Meehan, *Contemporary Political Thought: A Critical Study* (Dorsey Press, 1967), ch. 3. See also Robert A. Scott and Arnold R. Shore, *Why Sociology Does Not Apply: A Study of the Use of Sociology in Public Policy* (Elsevier, 1979).

7. Example taken from Eugene J. Meehan, *The Quality of Federal Policymaking: Programmed Disaster in Public Housing* (University of Missouri Press, 1979).

8. Eugene J. Meehan, *In Partnership with People: An Alternative Development Strategy* (U.S. Government Printing Office, 1979). The Inter-American Foundation, which is the topic of the monograph, was constituted by Congress in 1970 to learn how to do development.

9. There is a "social indicator" movement but its products are not useful for policymaking. For examples, see Raymond A. Bauer, ed., *Social Indicators* (MIT Press, 1966); Harvey A. Garn et al., *Social Indicator Models for Urban Policy: Five Specific Applications* (Urban Institute, 1973); Eleanor B. Sheldon and Wilbert E. Moore, eds., *Indicators of Social Change: Concepts and Measurements* (Russell Sage Foundation, 1968); and the *Social Indicators* series published by the U.S. Office of Management and Budget, or the parallel *Perspective Canada* series published by the Ministry of Supply and Services. For criticism, see Eugene J. Meehan, "The Social Indicator Movement," *Frontiers of Economics: 1975* (University Publications, Blacksburg, Va., 1976), pp. 27-43, or "Social Indicators and Policy Analysis," in Frank P. Scioli, Jr. and Thomas J. Cook, *Methodologies for Analyzing Public Policies* (Lexington Books, 1975), pp. 33-46.

10. William C. Thiesenhusen, "Reaching the Rural Poor and the Poorest: A Goal Unmet," in *International Perspectives in Rural Sociology,* ed. Howard Newby (John Wiley, 1978), p. 161. See also Cheryl A. Lassen, *Landlessness and Rural Poverty in Latin America: Trends and Policies Affecting Income and Employment* (Cornell University, Rural Development Committee, 1979), and Dennis A. Rondinelli, "Administration of Integrated Rural Development Policy: The Politics of Agrarian Reform in Developing Countries," *World Politics* 21, no. 3. (1979): 389-416.

11. See Lance T. LeLoup, *Budgetary Politics: Dollars, Deficits, Decisions* (King's Court Communications, 1977), and Aaron Wildavsky, *Budgeting: A Comparative Theory of Budgetary Processes* (Little, Brown, 1975).

How do the sciences, the empirical disciplines such as economics, contribute to reasoned policymaking? That question is the key to assessing economics' contribution to policymaking. A general answer is found in the linkage between the set of intellectual purposes from which the discussion began and the means of fulfilling them developed within the theory of knowledge. The heart of the intellectual enterprise is a reasoned effort to improve the human situation; that requires the capacity to anticipate or predict, to control, and to choose on reasoned grounds. Policies appear as part of reasoned choice, serving to apply a preference structure to a set of options. Reasoned choice is absolutely contingent on the ability to modify or control the future; both empirical and normative instruments are required. Presumably, the normative instruments (priorities) are the responsibility of those engaged in normative studies. Such tools cannot be generated from empirical or scientific inquiries as they are commonly understood. The sciences, or empirical disciplines, such as economics, contribute to policymaking by creating the instruments needed for systematically controlling events, and to a lesser extent by predicting them. A more detailed statement of the requirements and how they are fulfilled, specified in terms of the structures, processes, evidence, and argument required for satisfying the major purposes of inquiry, is contained in this chapter.

Although the prime need in policymaking is for instruments that can be used to control events, qualitative evaluation cannot focus on that aspect of inquiry alone. Production, criticism, and improvement of the instruments used to control events (to be called *theories* in the discussion that follows) depends upon a range of other products or instruments.[1] Perhaps the best way to demonstrate the extent of that contingency is to ask how human experience can be organized to produce the instruments required to exercise control over events in the environment reliably and accurately. It is quickly obvious that a range of intermediate structures and assumptions is required if an incoming flow of perceptions is to be transformed into an adequate and valid theory. Theories are the end result of a complex set of interactions; the quality of the theory is no better than the quality of its constituent elements. Criticism intended to improve policymaking, or even to improve theory, cannot focus exclusively at the level of theory. The quality of the contributing factors must also be examined. This chapter contains a brief sketch of the basic elements in theory development, emphasizing particularly the points that most often interfere with the proper operation of the theory, since they are of prime concern to the policymaker.

At the level of theory building and evaluation, science can contribute to policymaking at almost any point in a lengthy and complex sequence of interactions. But from the policymaker's point of view, that conception of contribution is too diffuse. It is conceivable that every inquiry in economics could be construed as a positive contribution to policymaking without collectively satisfying the necessary conditions for making a single reasoned policy. Everyone would make a contribution; no policy would emerge. The disciplinary product must be stronger, including adequate and significant theories. The contribution that economics can make to policymaking is therefore assessed primarily by reference to the theories it produces, though if theories are inadequate, the source of their inadequacy may be found in their constituent elements. Particular attention is given to conditions that will improve or interfere with the long range capacity of the discipline to generate theories that are adequate for making policies. In the present state of social science, that dimension of criticism is more important than detailed evaluation of the products of specific inquiries.

In the remainder of the chapter, then, the basic structures and processes used to organize human experience for the achievement of purposes in the environment will be examined systematically. The discussion begins with the basic building blocks, the concepts used to organize the incoming flow of raw perceptions, and concludes with a detailed examination of theories, the instruments used for controlling events in the environment. Four points are examined with respect to each structure: they are (1) the performance characteristics of the instrument—a useful technique for avoiding arguments about labels; (2) the set of assumptions on which the instrument depends; (3) the way experience is organized to produce the instrument; and (4) the evidence, argument, or justification needed for that type of instrument. The last two could perhaps be collapsed, but their separation calls attention to the role that application plays in developing and improving intellectual instruments and suggests reasons for rejecting any instrument not generated from or linked to experience.

## ORGANIZING EXPERIENCE: THE BASIC ELEMENTS

Knowledge, whether empirical or normative, consists in organized patterns of experience, or experience logically ordered and generalized. For all practical purposes, only two forms or patterns are required, though the underlying assumptions may vary. First, the characteristics or attributes of "things" observed in the environment are generalized from experience to form classifications; second, the relations among things, suitably limited, can be generalized to form static or dynamic patterns. In the process, a variety of logical or relational terms is employed, linguistic and syntactical requirements are satisfied and calculations are made within various logical structures. All such ancillary tools must be taken for granted here as they are much too complex to be dealt with briefly.

### CONCEPTS

The initial organization of perceptions entering the central nervous system is made with *concepts* or classifications, usually defined as a way of organizing perceptions. A concept identifies a class

of things in the observed world that can be separated from the
rest of the world, bounded, and treated as entities. The meaning
of a concept is found in the set of attributes that defines member-
ship in the class to which it refers. Some concepts, such as pure
colors, are considered "simple" and nonanalyzable, but most are
complex, defined with the use of other concepts. More formally,
a concept is defined by a set of propositions that state the distributed
properties of a class, the properties shared by every class member.

Classification depends on an analytically straightforward process,
though it requires creativity or generalization. Perceptions are dis-
criminated, grouped or organized to identify stable and consistent
patterns within the environment. The boundaries of the "thing"
are imposed by the observer, but not arbitrarily; the observer may
decide that the tiger's tail goes with the rest of the animal but nature
supplies reasons for accepting the relation that are difficult to ignore.
The process depends on observation of class members, recording
what is observed as descriptions, then generalizing shared attributes
in suitable form. In effect, a classification stores information about
a particular class of things. If the classification is large and rich,
it can be subdivided; that makes the storage system more accurate
and manageable. Analytically if not historically, the class member
precedes the classification and there must be at least two members
to have a classification. A single thing can have its attributes generalized, of course, and over time, attributes can be multiplied,
refined, and made more accurate. But the adequacy or usefulness
of a classification depends on the purpose for which it can be used.
Classifications can be generated without any specific purpose in
mind, but the dimensions of behavior or appearance considered
important enough to include in the classification must then be decided on other grounds. The results are sometimes peculiar and
even incongruous—books about trees that say nothing of their
usefulness as wood, for birds, or even provision of shade, for example.

The justification for accepting a concept or classification will
refer to observations of class members. Since it is usually impossible
to observe every member of a class, the selection of class properties
(which are generalized and hence must be assumed) is problematic.
In principle at least, the next member of the class observed could
be different from the others. That happens occasionally in almost
every field and a decision must then be made whether the exception should be treated as an aberration or whether the attributes
of the class should be changed. Europeans assumed for a very long

time that all swans were white, for example, but creatures were found in Australia that were clearly swans but black in color. The classification was amended and the birds were included in the swan family. Classifications generalize observations, more or less accurately, hence are limited by what is observed; they involve creativity and judgment but content cannot be extended without observational warrant.

Concepts are an important source of error and inadequacy in the instruments used in policymaking. The two most common faults are vagueness and ambiguity. A concept is *vague* if meaning and application cannot be established; a concept is *ambiguous* if it has two or more meanings and the correct one cannot be established in context. Both errors occur frequently in inquiry, particularly in social science. One solution to the conceptual problem, often recommended for social science, is to follow the physical sciences and adopt technical terms or standard concepts. Some standardization would probably be beneficial, but wholesale conversion to standard concepts would be premature, for both practical and theoretical reasons. In practical terms, the institutional arrangements needed to develop and maintain standard concepts are not available. Moreover, the root concepts probably could not be agreed by present inquirers, even in limited fields. The theoretical objections are much more serious. Development of standard concepts suggests they should be used in inquiry, and that the resulting knowledge would be significant. It is almost impossible to justify such assumptions within most of the social sciences. Moreover, opponents of standardization argue with some cogency that most of the great advances in human knowledge have entailed a major reconceptualization of the field—Einstein's contributions to physics are notable but not unique in this respect. Premature standardization could therefore be expected to impede the very freedom to speculate and test that reconceptualization requires. Despite such arguments, critics of standardization usually recognize the need to stabilize and improve the available concepts. That has opened the door to serious abuse in some fields, notably economics, where the practice of developing formal or abstract models and conducting inquiry within that framework has become commonplace. When the models are based on nominally defined symbols, as occurs generally in economics, the practice is wholly unacceptable, for reasons to be detailed in due course.

*Definitions* The meaning of concepts is contained in their definitions, and definitions are a major source of misunderstanding and theoretical weakness in social science. There are various ways to create a definition for a concept or term; the acceptability of the result depends on the purpose of the user. The widespread belief that terms can be defined in any way an inquirer chooses so long as they are used consistently is seriously mistaken. It holds for one special class of definitions, which cannot be used in empirical inquiry. A quick summary of the major types of definitions will serve to clarify the problem involved.

The definitions found in dictionaries are merely a record of current usage, updated periodically. The quality of the definition is not assessed; several meanings are given, usually in order of preference. Such lexical definitions can be narrowed by the use of precising terms, say by restricting the meanings of "political party member" to persons who contribute time or money to a party organization. Precising definitions are useful so long as the restricted meaning is adhered to rigorously. The dangers, readily seen with respect to such usage as the definition of policy developed here, are of two sorts. First, the user may intermingle the restricted meaning with everyday meaning creating an insoluble ambiguity for the reader or listener. On the other hand, if the reader forgets to maintain the restricted meaning, in either all or part of the material, the same ambiguous effect follows. To avoid confusion, those who use special meanings usually reiterate them periodically, as a reminder to the reader—and that too can be very annoying to those who remember the special definition perfectly well.

For criticizing the contribution that economics can make to reasoned policymaking, the most important distinction to be made lies between *real* or lexical definitions and *nominal* or stipulative definitions.[2] Economists rarely make the distinction, and that omission seriously reduces the usefulness of their products in policymaking. The error is easily made; the distinction is complex and not usually noted, even in methodological texts. For inquiry directed to the fulfillment of human purposes, separation of the two types of definitions is crucial. A real definition is based on experience and refers to observation; every concept must have a real definition, as must relational terms used in descriptions. Since real definitions refer to observation and experience, they can be tested, and their accuracy and adequacy can be disputed. The meaning of such terms as mumps or measles, for example, cannot be defined arbitrarily even though the arbitrary definition is used consistently.

Terms that are defined nominally do not refer to observation and experience; they refer instead to other sets of symbols. To quote Robert Bierstedt, who called attention to the need for clarification many years ago, a nominal definition is "a declaration of intention to use a certain word or phrase as a substitute for another word or phrase."[3] Since nominal definitions do not refer to experience, they cannot be challenged or tested. Terms so defined are only replacements for other terms; they have no further meaning. The term used and the term replaced can be decided by the user with complete freedom. There is, however, a price. Propositions that depend on nominally defined terms are absolutely unrelated to the world of experience and they cannot be used in argument or as a base for inference. They are nevertheless essential for systematic inquiry. All of the terms in mathematics are nominally defined, to take an important example. Nominal definitions offer a means for simplifying problems since they allow substitution of a single symbol for a complex set of propositions. They also avoid the pejorative overtones associated with sensitive issues, thus furthering objective discussion. Finally, nominal definitions are the only means available for introducing new concepts into inquiry; so long as they are converted into real definitions in due course, they are invaluable.

Unfortunately, real and nominal definitions are very easily interchanged and the result is disastrous. Most commonly, terms in everyday use are given nominal definitions which are exchanged for everyday meanings during the course of the argument, particularly in the conclusions. Abuse is located by substituting definition for term where it occurs. Real definitions are reversible *simpliciter* without modifying the meaning of the proposition in which they appear. Technically, the relationship established is class equivalence; that requires evidence that is not formal or logical, evidence that comes from experience. An example from economics may help to clarify the distinction and illlustrate the dangers involved. The term *oligarchy,* which means despotic rule by a small clique, is given a nominal definition in the following quotation:

At this point, we introduce the concept of oligarchy. Suppose that everyone in society outside a given set S of individuals is indifferent between alternatives x and y. Social choice between x and y is then determined by the members of set S. An oligarchy relative to S is the smallest subset V of members such that, if x is preferred to y by all the oligarchs, it is also preferred by the society.[4]

Now, that is not an adequate real definition of oligarchy, whose meaning has roots that extend to classic Greece and beyond. If the conclusions are stated using the term oligarchy, as actually occurs, any reader familiar with the real definition will certainly be misled. As Bierstedt notes, a conceptual scheme is only a language and can be stipulated, but a substantive theory is propositional and contains statements about the observable world. The conclusions drawn from a substantive theory will incorporate truth claims with reference to the world. The concepts employed, therefore, must have real definitions. Using nominal definitions in such cases is precisely equivalent to using false premises in a theoretical structure intended for use in policymaking.

*Indicators and Measurements.* Every concept must have some set of directly observable indicators that cue the correct use of the concept and provide a way of measuring its value or magnitude. In some cases, one of the defining attributes of the class will also serve as indicator and measuring base for the class. But in more complex cases, indicators are linked to the concept through a set of interlocking theories. For example, the connection between visible splashes on the surface of a lake and the fish feeding beneath the surface is established through theories. Or, the connection between the friction between molecules in a liquid, which is called viscosity, and the rate of flow of the liquid, must also be established by a theoretical chain. The meaning of the concept is wider than the indicator, as temperature implies more than the length of the column of mercury used to measure it.

From a different perspective, an indicator is a base from which diagnosis can determine the proper concept to use in observation. The usefulness of the indicator can vary greatly, depending on the quality of the linking theory. Indicators for such concepts as recession may be extremely difficult to find. Simply increasing the number of indicators or the precision of the measurements does not guarantee better diagnosis. That problem, however, is best left for discussion when forecasts and theories are being examined.

Very broadly, measurement means observation, the production of information. The kind of measurements made determine the amount of information produced. As in thermodynamics, no more can be taken out of observation than was put in by the observer. Many of the difficulties over measurement refer to the validity of inferences drawn formally or statistically from a given body of information. Propositions based on the results of such mathematical manipulations must be justified in the first instance by showing that the inferred conclusions were actually contained in the data. Put another way, the measurements used must satisfy the axioms of the mathematical apparatus used in analysis. In the social sciences, that rule is frequently violated. In the discussion that follows, the validity of statistical applications is assumed but in real world studies that would be unwise. The computer making calculations deals solely with the numbers and not meaning; it can explore the content of a proposition but cannot augment it. If the results of calculation are used as evidence to support a proposition, that causes no serious problems; but if conclusions are regarded as validated by statistical treatment, then their content must be available in the original information. The two positions are frequently confused in the social sciences.

DESCRIPTIONS

Concepts are the basic organizing instrument in empirical inquiry. Combined with observations, concepts are used to produce descriptions, which are the fundamental information base from which all other intellectual instruments are developed. In that sense, a description is the most basic form of organized human experience. They are so important in scientific development that the absence of a rich supply of descriptions can be taken as a good indicator of a relatively weak discipline. Despite their importance, descriptions are not adequately treated in most approaches to inquiry. They are far more complex and less certain than is implied in such everyday usage as references to "hard facts."

To describe, one or more concepts, and an appropriate number of logical or relational terms, are taken to the environment and their values are measured and recorded. Structurally, a description consists of a set of variables, including their interrelations, whose values are fixed by observation for a specific time and place. Descriptions are not precisely analogous to photographs. In a camera, the transformation of external events into the picture that appears on the film depends on rules that are fixed and known. The structure is not selective within the limits of its construction. Descriptive content incorporates a human judgment, a selection of factors, and the basis of selection is always uncertain in some degree. Put another way, description requires the application of classifications;

they contain assertions to the effect that a member of some class was observed at a particular time and place. Such assertions depend on diagnosis or judgment, and are therefore problematic. The cognitive status of descriptions is not accurately conveyed by such phrases as "hard facts." Descriptions involve assumptions and judgments, and therefore require justification. They are neither self-evident nor self-justifying. The simplest illustration of the need for interpretation or theoretical justification in observation is found in the familiar illusion of bending created when a stick is partly immersed in water. The stick appears bent but that is not usually asserted as fact, even though it appears in an observation.

Despite such technical limitations, sound descriptions are the foundation stone for every knowledge system and good reasons can be given for accepting or rejecting most descriptive accounts. Merely employing the descriptive form is not enough, however; descriptive propositions must make sense in terms of current knowledge. Assertions such as "The goat flew to the top of a nearby tree," would certainly be rejected. If concepts are clear, indicators are adequate, measurements are accurate and reliable, and observations are properly made, then description is probably the strongest form of knowledge available, and the strongest evidence that can be offered to support other propositions. To that extent, systematic analysis fully confirms common sense.

Either the accuracy or the adequacy of descriptive accounts can affect the value and usefulness of instruments based upon them. Accuracy is a function of the concepts, measurements, and observational techniques employed; adequacy depends upon the purposes for which the description is intended. Both are important to the policymaker. The causes and effects of descriptive inaccuracy are well known and need not be rehearsed here. The influence of subjectivity on descriptive accuracy and reliability is particularly important in social science because the techniques used in physical science to increase accuracy are not applicable. Moreover, measuring tools create their own problems, for instruments can observe only the elements included in the design, therefore design flaws translate into either inaccuracy or inadequacy. The most flexible and adaptive of all measuring instruments is, of course, the human observer. The human internal measurement "program" can bring into play virtually all of past intellectual experience with suitable prompting.

No television camera at a sports event can transmit everything that a trained observer actually "sees," if only because the human observer is a cumulator while the camera can only deal with the here and now. The price of such flexibility, however, is greater uncertainty, for the human observer may omit and the camera cannot.

The adequacy of a description depends on the user's purpose. An account of a damaged automobile adequate for police records will not do for the mechanic estimating repair costs even though it is quite accurate. A complete description is impossible in principle; every description is a selection from a potentially infinite set of alternative accounts. The selection actually incorporated into a description will therefore serve some purposes and not others. An analogy to maps is heuristically useful. Like maps, descriptions can be enriched by increasing the amount and kind of information included. Ultimately, the procedure fails, for the costs of production and use rise to a point where it becomes cheaper to produce a new description than to explore the complexities of what is recorded and select what purpose requires.

The significance of descriptive adequacy for the user is also well illustrated using the analogy to maps. It would be pointless to purchase a map that did not contain needed information, however accurate it might be. The actual content of a description is limited by the available supply of concepts, the content of the environment, the observer's purposes, and the theoretical structure used to select salient dimensions of the environment to record. What is not present cannot be recorded, of course, but the guiding framework may suggest that the absence of some element should be noted. The importance of *purpose* in description flows from the need for descriptive adequacy. Without a purpose, the observer has no reason for including or excluding information beyond tradition, personal feelings, or happenstance. Purposeless description is like an excursion in verbal photography using a partially covered lens, and directing the camera more or less randomly. The result is unlikely to be useful for any purpose because those who wish to use it cannot tell whether the absence of any reference to a particular object is accidental or deliberate. Much the same dilemma occurs when historical records are created or studied without a clear purpose in mind.

In the wider context of the whole knowledge system, descriptions are ubiquitous. A change, which is the central focus in forecasting and theorizing, is an inference from two or more descriptions of the same thing at two points in time. An expectation refers to the content of an as yet unmade description, carried out under appropriate conditions. To control the environment means in effect to produce a future that will match a specified descriptive account. A choice leads to the situation contained in one description rather than the situation contained in one or more others. And, since a description consists of a selection of variables whose values are fixed by observation, which can be symbolized very efficiently, descriptions are particularly useful for demonstrating the functions performed by the various intellectual instruments and the reason they are able to carry them out. Finally, familiarity with descriptive accounts of phenomena, knowing "what is the case," is an essential prerequisite to all theorizing, policymaking, or evaluation.

*Conceptual Frameworks* Humans do not observe randomly, in most cases, nor are concepts randomly distributed across cognitive maps within the intellectual apparatus. Instead, concepts are clustered or grouped to form what are here called conceptual frameworks—sets of concepts that tend to be used together for a common task. They are theoretical derivatives, or precursors to theory, linking together the sets of concepts that presumably relate to the purposes for which the framework is used. What identifies the dentist, economist, or electrician at work is the conceptual framework employed. Learning the framework needed for specific tasks is an important part of education. Selecting the appropriate framework is essential for learning what is going on and thereby being in a position to assist with the task or learn from it. Lack of a conceptual framework appropriate to the task, or use of the wrong framework, can have extremely serious consequences. The automobile driver who vacillates between conceptual frameworks while driving is a case in point. All conceptual frameworks incorporate normative considerations either directly or indirectly. Those used in policymaking, or for creating instruments used in policymaking, must include the normatively significant dimensions of the situation to which they apply if they are to fulfill basic requirements.

Conceptual frameworks determine the significance attached to specific perceptions, and thus control the decision to react to them or record them in a description. A physician responds quickly to the sight of blood spurting from an artery, the automobile driver to the sight of an automobile in the wrong lane or a child along the roadside. Conceptual frameworks are rudimentary theories, sets of relations based on experience but perhaps not fully and completely linked. Their availability is a good indicator of disciplinary capacity. There are few useful criteria for criticizing such frameworks, however, nor is their development and improvement well understood.

The corollaries to conceptual weakness, or the absence of adequate conceptual frameworks are highly visible, and readily illustrated from social science. Inquiry tends to be directed by fad and tradition rather than normative purpose or theoretical needs. Subfields within the discipline show little or no integration. Inquirers depend heavily on established information sources and standard data-processing procedures. The results of inquiry rarely find use in everyday affairs. Of course, well-established conceptual frameworks may also impede disciplinary improvement. For as such frameworks are internalized and refined, modification and innovation become increasingly difficult to procure. In thinking, as in travel, the well-worn trails are most often used; that may facilitate the journey but it tends to discourage the search for alternatives. The young, who have not yet developed "grooves" for their intellectual forays, understandably dominate creativity in such fields as mathematics and science. Awareness of current practice, and habitual questioning of established practice, is the best antidote to excessive reliance upon established conceptualizations, but they are much easier to discuss in principle than to apply in practice.

## GENERATING EXPECTATIONS

To expect or anticipate means to predict that some situation or event not yet observed can or will be observed in future. Structurally, an expectation states the content of a future description made under specified limiting conditions. Usually, expectations refer to the future but it is often useful to generate expectations about the unobserved past, in effect to predict that some event in the past had a particular effect. Statements of expectations can make use of a range of verbs, of course, and need not include "predict" or "expect." All expectations are in some degree problematic since they are inferences from a set of assumptions combined with observations. Predictions cannot satisfy the requirements for reasoned policymaking; they can suggest a need for action but not the action required.

If no justification is demanded, statements containing expectations or predictions are easily produced. But in the absence of justification, such propositions are merely prophecy. Of course, some prophets are more reliable than others, but the quality of a prophecy cannot be criticized apart from the person who produced it. In one limited sense, the quality of a prediction is independent of its justification but that quality cannot be tested until the predicted situation is available to observation. For reasoned action or policymaking, expectations must be justified *before* production or use.

Expectations that can be justified are produced using instruments created by organizing human experience to form patterns in much the same way that other intellectual purposes are fulfilled. An observation is made, the pattern is assumed, and the implications of the combination of pattern and observation become the substance of the expectation. For all intellectual instruments, the general rule for criticism is that the instrument must connect two or more observations or observables. A structure that generates expectations out of its own internal operations is intellectually worthless—many of Freud's "theories" exemplify the error. Such expectation-generators can be tested in the same manner as any other source of prophecies; they cannot be improved. Valid intellectual patterns link an observed cue to an expectation that can also be observed through an appropriate set of rules or logic. Structurally, the rules relate the values taken by some finite set of variables at two points of time. The selection of variables can be altered by reducing values to zero or changing value from zero to some positive measure. Both of the observables must lie within the pattern, or be incorporated into the rules. Every instrument used to generate justified expectations must satisfy these basic requirements.

Both patterns that state the attributes of classes and patterns that link or relate classes can be used to make forecasts. The concept or classification, which is the primary instrument for organizing perceptions, can also be used to generate expectations. The second type of forecasting device links two observed changes in the environment by rule. In each case, evaluation or criticism of predictions proceeds in two stages: first, it must be demonstrated that once the initial observation is made, accepting the pattern entails the prediction—a question of logic; second, the instrument used to make the prediction must be validated or justified, and be shown to apply to the situation.

PREDICTING WITH CLASSIFICATIONS

The predictive power of a classification depends on the way in which it is created. Each concept or classification incorporates the generalized shared attributes of an identifiable class of things and can be tested against observations of the class. Structurally, a classification consists of a set of variables that identify shared attributes and a set of rules that specify the limiting values for each of the variables. The class "cats," for example, will be defined by a set of rules (R) that state the specific limits on size, shape, color, behavioral attributes, and so on. In symbolic notation, classifications appear as follows:

$$[ (V_1 \; V_2 \; V_3 \; V_4 \ldots V_n ) \qquad (R_1 \; R_2 \; R_3 \; R_4 \ldots R_n ) ]$$

The content of the classification must be determined from and tested against observation; it cannot be postulated. Any observed entity that shares all of the defining attributes of the class must be accepted as a member of that class. Each class member will have all of the enumerated attributes. Minor deviations or aberrations can safely be ignored, but serious anomalies indicate an inadequate classification.

Given a well-established classification, application is a fairly simple task. Use is triggered by observation. For example, if a bird some eighteen inches long with black body and flaming red crest is observed in the central United States, it can be identified confidently as a pileated woodpecker—the only crested bird of that size in the area. That assumption made, logical extension generates the expectation that the remaining attributes of the class will be observed under appropriate conditions—it will make a particular kind of nest, migrate in season, and so on. If a diagnosis is not made until *all* of the attributes of the class have been observed, either the observer lacks skill or the classification is inadequate and must be improved. The logic used to project the expectation is elementary:

Established:    All members of class X have properties p

Assumed:        A (observed) is a member of class X

Prediction:     A will have all of the properties of class X

The expectation is the sum of the established properties of the class minus properties already observed. That use of classification provides a very good example of the power of tautologies. If the classification has been properly developed and tested, the observation was accurate, the identification correct, and the logical operations correctly performed, the expectation is justified and should be fulfilled. The procedure is very common in every area of life. Medical diagnosis and treatment relies on the same procedure; so does the purchase of graded meats in the butcher's shop, the use of psychological tests, or even the rating of movies in terms of appropriateness for younger audiences.

The reason why good classifications are able to generate accurate and reliable expectations is found in the way that classes are created and tested. Classifications store generalized information about an identified class of things. Their development begins with the entities classified and proceeds by observation, location of shared attributes, and generalization of those shared attributes. The procedure creates a real definition for the class, based on an examination of particular class members. Observation continues to a point where only minor variations appear in successive cases. In principle, the definition of the class remains problematic and incomplete, but in practice classifications can be extremely rich, accurate, and reliable.

The importance of purpose in the environment to the quality of the intellectual instrument produced is readily illustrated with respect to classifications. In principle, any singular event can be classified in an infinite number of different ways; there is no formal or procedural way out of the infinite regress. An external criterion is needed to justify asserting that the result is adequate and inquiry can be halted. Accuracy is an insufficient criterion, for that would be like evaluating a phonograph record solely on the basis of surface quality. And in any case, accuracy is always indeterminate at some level of precision in measurement; measuring capacity ultimately breaks down and the act of measuring interferes with the thing being measured. An external purpose makes it possible to identify the relevant dimensions of the class of things being observed. Birds may be classified as food, as esthetic objects, or as nuisances, for example, and the characteristics included in the classification system will be different in each case. One of the more curious aspects of natural science is the extent to which naturalists have managed to evade responsibility for the widespread ignorance of the social worth of birds and other wild creatures slaughtered in such vast numbers over the past two centuries, even though they are presumptively the primary source of information about such matters.

Expectations produced with classifications are justified or criticized by referring to three basic points: the adequacy of the instrument, the validity of the application or diagnosis; the correctness of the formal inference. Since the elements have already been covered, an example may serve to bring them together and show how they work in the particular case. Assume that Smith observes a peculiar lump on Jones's body, diagnoses a particular form of cancer, assumes that the cancer is quick-acting and lethal, and predicts that Jones will perish shortly. Is that expectation warranted? Jones, at least, will be deeply concerned with the quality of the intellectual performance. What procedures should he follow to check the prediction? First, obviously, he can confirm the presence of the lump. If it is present, the next step is to test the diagnosis. Is a lump of that kind a reliable indicator of the form of cancer in question? That judgment requires knowledge of the theoretical links between concept and indicator and can be obtained by consulting an expert in the field. Assuming the diagnosis is confirmed, the next question has to do with the attributes of the disease, the content of the classification. Is it really fatal in all cases? That too depends on experience and requires the kind of knowledge available to a competent and experienced physician. Suppose further than this question too is answered affirmatively. Jones has contracted a disease that in the past has been fatal within a few months of diagnosis. Is Jones doomed? The logical aspect of the prediction remains to be checked:

Established:　All persons with cancer A perish quickly
Established:　Jones has contracted cancer A
Prediction:　Jones will perish quickly

Unfortunately for Jones, the formal inference is correct. There remains one last hope. All such predictions are in some degree problematic. Death is not an absolute certainty. Jones could be the first exception to the pattern of past experience. It may be scant consolation, and as a matter of strategy, Jones would perhaps be wise to wind up any pending business, but it offers one faint hope that Jones might wish to retain.

An everyday illustration of this kind raises in microcosm all of the fundamentals of applied science. Two points in the process are crucial, the identification of the class (diagnosis) and the justification provided for accepting a specified set of class attributes. There is no formal solution to either problem. Jones could provide evidence that would justify a change in the defining characteristics of the disease from which he suffered. Experts can disagree profoundly on diagnosis as well as treatment, even in medicine. What is surprising is not the presence of such controversy but the strength of the opinions held with respect to very problematic outcomes. Of course, the committed do not consider the outcome to which commitment is made to be problematic—which is why such commitments are inappropriate in scientific inquiry. The Scotch verdict, No decision possible on the basis of the available evidence, should probably be heard far more often than is actually the case, particularly in social science.

Even when the experts are open-minded, and the situation is neutral, diagnosis can be a formidable problem. Consider a physician in antiquity who knows nothing of appendicitis but is very familiar with acute indigestion and constipation. The symptoms of the two illnesses are roughly the same—nausea, stomach pains, vomiting, and so on. The usual treatment for intestinal blockage is a strong laxative. But administering a laxative to a person with appendicitis can lead to rupture of the appendix, peritonitis, and eventual death. What would that physician make of the fatal outcome? Would it be included in the classification of acute indigestion? What reason would there be for the physician to do anything different? The diagnosis tends to be self-confirming once made: some persons afflicted with acute indigestion actually die of it. How can the vicious circle be broken? Again, there is no formal solution but without awareness that such possibilities *may* occur, there is little likelihood that the misclassification will be detected.

PREDICTING WITH FORECASTS

A classification generates expectations by organizing past experience with bounded entities into generalized patterns. Assuming the generalized pattern, and combining it with an observation, allows a formal inference of the remaining attributes of the class member. A more flexible and accurate predicting device is created if two or more classes of things are linked through a generalized pattern created out of experience in the same manner. Such patterns are particularly useful for predicting changes in the environment reliably and accurately.

Two types of instruments, identical in structure but incorporating different assumptions, can be created by generalizing the relations among observables. Each consists of two or more variables and a set of rules linking their values—plus the limiting conditions to be satisfied prior to application. One instrument, labeled a *forecast,* generalizes correlations in the values of some set of variables under specified limits; the second, labeled a *theory,* generalizes a causal relation between the variables or incorporates a causal assumption. The discussion here will refer only to forecasts. A theory can, however, be used to produce a justified expectation with respect to the future.

A forecast generalizes past correlations between two or more variables and nothing more. There is no assumption that the variables are causally linked and no implication that deliberately changing the value of one will produce a predictable change in the other. Indeed, since the correlations usually generalize observations of the drift flow of events, interference with the flow may invalidate the forecast. A puppy that drinks readily from a bowl of water if left alone may refuse to drink if pressed to do so by the owner. Application of a forecast is cued by an observation. When one of the variables included in the forecast is observed, and the limiting conditions are met, the rule incorporated in the forecast will generate an expectation with respect to the value of the other variable. That meaning corresponds fairly well to current usage, particularly in such areas as weather forecasting.

Forecasts have only limited utility in policymaking because they do not provide a basis for action. Predictions based on past correlations suggest areas where human intervention is required but not the appropriate intervention strategy. Since there is no causal relation assumed, forecasts cannot be tested experimentally. Without the causal assumption, there is no logical relation between action and expectation.

In everyday affairs, forecasts are easy to construct and apply, readily justified and extremely useful.[5] Indeed, the principle of forecasting is more commonly used than the label. For example, if past experience supports a simple general statement such as "These flowers (B) bloom about two weeks after those flowers (A)," the basic requirements of forecasting are already satisfied. The limiting clause *(ceteris paribus)* needed to handle contingencies may be suppressed but is usually clearly understood. Limited but reliable expectations can be generated by applying the instrument. When flowers of type A are observed to bloom, that cues application of the forecast "B blooms two weeks after A," generating a prediction in the form, "Flowers (B) will bloom in about two weeks." Precisely the same principles are used in the more complex calculations on which predictions about economic activity depend. The overall procedure is by now familiar: experience with particular cases is generalized into a pattern or set of rules; an observation cues use of the pattern; applied to the observation, the pattern logic produces an expectation or prediction. The justification for assuming the forecast is found in past experience with the two observables.

When the forecasts are developed deliberately and consciously, as in business, the purpose to be served will be specified quite precisely. In a typical case, a prediction of the future value of some target variable such as monthly sales or material costs is requested. Some other variable must be found whose value has changed following the same pattern as the value of the target variable. The variables need not be related either conceptually or theoretically, and that gives rise to the widespread but mistaken belief that forecasting is possible using "false" assumptions. So long as the values of the variables covary regularly over time, and the target variable lags behind by some suitable interval, an instrument can be created that will predict the future value of the target variable from the current value of the other variable in the set. In some cases, future values can be projected from the past history of the variable being predicted. That is, if sales have increased by 10 percent each year for several years, a rough estimate of future sales is obtained by assuming that the rate of increase will continue. The justification for the assumption will begin with the historical record, perhaps cite the absence of any known interferences, indicate that the factors that influence sales positively have altered as in previous years, and thus create a body of evidence to support the prediction. More commonly, a forecaster locates a bellwether, a variable whose values change in the same direction and ratio as the target variable with an appropriate time lead. The past history of the relation is generalized to a formula, tested against historical data, then used to make future projections. Most of econometrics depends on that principle. Over time, the predicting formula can be refined or complicated by adding limiting conditions and so on. If the activity predicted is relatively stable, reliability can be quite remarkable, even if human behavior is involved. The National Safety Council's predictions of traffic fatalities on national holidays is a case in point.

Determining reliability in advance of use is the most difficult part of forecasting. The only available basis for justification is past history. The first step is to demonstrate that the forecast would have produced reliable predictions had it been employed earlier. The evidence is strengthened if there were no counterexamples. Other things equal, and they seldom are, the longer the time frame, and the larger the number of cases involved, the more worthy the evidence. A number of separate predictions can be made for the same event, using different variables in each case. If they coincide, that strengthens the justification and can improve reliability. Finally, known or suspected causal relations can be incorporated into the forecast, providing additional reason for expecting the event—some of the necessary conditions may be known or none of the known inhibitors may be present.

From the point of view of the policymaker, a forecast has two primary dimensions. The first is not, as might be supposed, accuracy or reliability. Instead, the policymaker looks first to see if the predicted events have significance. If the temperature in the antarctic region is expected to fall some 5° F. below normal in the coming winter, the policymaker wants to know first whether that has any direct or indirect consequences for the population that is his prime concern. If it does not, accuracy and reliability are a matter of indifference. If the outcome can be linked to significant changes in the human condition (perhaps to major increases in fuel costs or even to fuel shortages,) the quality of the prediction, and its implications, will be more fully explored. The forecast does not suggest a need for action directly; it does so in combination with a normative system. Nor does it provide an intervention strategy for changing the situation. That requires a theory. A predicted outbreak of influenza will certainly lead to collective action but the actions taken are derived from the available medical theories and not from the forecasts used to predict the epidemic.

## CONTROLLING THE ENVIRONMENT: THEORIES

In reasoned policymaking, empirical and normative instruments are combined to produce a guide to action that will lead to the preferred outcome from a given selection. On the normative side, instruments are needed that can identify and justify the preferred outcome within the available options. Empirical inquiry must supply instruments that can both project the range of outcomes from which a choice is made, and suggest an intervention strategy for achieving the preferred outcome. The analytic order is not binding historically. Reasoned and corrigible policies depend absolutely on the ability to exercise some control over future events. The instrument that makes control over future events *possible in principle* will be called a *theory*. That definition corresponds reasonably well with conceptions of theory in philosophy of science but not with all of them, mainly because of the emphasis placed here on controlling events, and the assumed causal relation that entails. On the conception of theory required for policymaking, the instrument can answer three kinds of questions: What caused an event to occur? How can that situation be changed? and What changes will follow from that action? The meaning of cause is simply a constant conjunction of action and consequence, but the emphasis on *action and effect* is essential. The structures and processes required to answer those questions, and the way in which human experience can be organized to produce the instrument required, will be examined below in more detail.

Control over events is achieved through the same basic procedure used to satisfy any human purpose in the environment. Experience is organized and generalized to create a structure or pattern; an observation is made; the pattern is assumed; the implications are calculated. Because of the assumed causal relation between variables, the instrument can be tested experimentally. Structurally, a theory is identical to a forecast, consisting in a set of two or more variables whose values are linked by one or more rules. The causal assumption, which may be unidirectional or reciprocal, implies that deliberately changing the value of one variable in the theory will cause the other to change according to the rules. A theory is a calculus for action, a device for linking action to consequences. The limiting conditions are an integral part of the overall structure. The theory must hold only in principle; the technology required to implement it need not be available.

The crux of a theory, the source of its power, is the assumed causal relation between the variables; it fulfills the logical requirements for the instrument. Both the strong and weak forms of causality can be used to develop an adequate theory. If the necessary conditions for an event to occur can be located in experience, a theory can be created in the form, "No X unless Y under conditions C." Such instruments cannot suggest a way of producing the event through human action but they do provide a strategy for acting to prevent occurrence. For example, if a temperature below 32° F. is a necessary condition for changing water from liquid to solid form, then freezing can be prevented by maintaining a temperature above that point. A much stronger theory is possible if the sufficient conditions for an event can be determined, though it is correspondingly more difficult to create and to justify. Such theories serve as a base for positive action, can be used to produce a preferred outcome, say curing a patient by administering an antibiotic. Usage varies on this point but it is helpful to keep the two types of causal relations separated. In either case, the phenomenon to be controlled, which is normally shown as an entailment of a theory, must actually appear within the set of variables that make up the theory. Once a theory is established, any time the selection of variables included in the theory appears in observation, and the limiting conditions are satisfied, the rules of interaction are expected to hold. Further, any combination of values for the variables that can be produced by combining observation and the rules of interaction should be possible in observation. Theories are limited to real possibilities; they cannot project a set of permutations that will include empty cells as well as the results of observation and calculation. If that were allowed, which implication would be acceptable?

THE LOGIC OF THEORIES

   Organizing a body of experience into a generalized pattern has the effect of applying a logic or calculus to a set of observations. In that sense, theorizing is nothing more than the application of logic or mathematics to the real world. The calculus is the engine that pulls the chain of inferences; it supplies the dynamic for the theoretical enterprise. Logic or mathematics has the capacity to generate and verify implications, or more precisely, to explore the content of a set of general propositions. Once the basic axioms of the system have been accepted, the structure has the power to force agreement with the conclusions on pain of self-contradiction. To harness that calculating power to observation, the formal symbols in the logic, which are nominally defined and have meaning only within the logic, must be given empirical meaning. The connection is established through rules of transformation. The calculations are made only within the logic. The results are transferred to observation if the transformation rules are properly made. The ultimate justification for the transformation rules is pragmatic but in an ongoing field of inquiry other reasons can usually be offered for accepting a proposed application of logic before it has actually been made. Some of the procedures involved, and the limits they impose on theorizing and use of theories, are worth noting specifically.

   Formally, a logic is a set of symbols whose meaning is contained in a set of nominal definitions and a set of axioms that stipulate the operations that can be performed with the symbols. Usually, a theory will be stated within one of the available logics—algebra or the calculus, for example—but there is no reason why a new logical structure cannot be produced for a particular purpose so long as it qualifies as a genuine logic. In the notation employed here, theories take the following basic form:

$$\left( \begin{array}{c} V_1 \ V_2 \ V_3 \ \ldots \ V_n \\ R_1 \ R_2 \ \ldots \ R_n \end{array} \right) \supset \emptyset$$

A set of limiting conditions will always be specified, though if the theory is well known, they may be omitted or suppressed. The curved brackets indicate that the set is closed and calculable. Any change in the value of one variable in the set can be accounted for completely by changes in the values of the other variables, given the rules of interaction. Put another way, the effect of changing one variable in the set can be calculated fully and precisely. In some limited cases, the antecedent change responsible for an observed change can be identified, though the justification required for such structures is very demanding. In the discussion that follows, the validity of calculation is assumed; in real cases, it would have to be verified.

The critical point in the use of theory is the transfer of calculations from logic to real world action. Creating a logical structure and identifying the symbols with observables is only the beginning of the process. The heart of the logic is not the set of symbols but the set of rules of interaction that link the values of the variables; the symbols are actually contained in those rules or they are otiose. To apply the logic to observations, the relations specified in the rules must fit the events observed in the environment. The system, considered dynamically and not cross-sectionally, must be isomorphic to observation. Change must be matched by change. For example, the rule of acceleration in the Laws of Motion must fit the observed behavior of freely falling bodies. Isomorphism refers to the content of the rules of interaction and not merely to an identified set of observables.

For the policymaker's purposes, isomorphism between the dynamics of logical structure and observation is clearly essential. The use of "false" axioms or rules of interaction would be nonsensical. Even in forecasting, there is no possibility of incorporating a genuinely false axiom into the structure. The variables in a forecast need not be related causally, but the rules used to project future states must generalize past observations of the relations among those same variables. If the rule incorporates a false statement about those relations, there would be no reason to expect an accurate prediction, and no justification for accepting the forecast. The apparent falseness of the axiom refers to the causal relation and not to historical covariance. Of course, logical structures that incorporate relations known to be false can be created and some of their implications calculated, generating "predictions." But the cognitive status of these implications differs radically from the predictions generated by genuine forecasts. They are only pseudo-predictions because they do not refer to the real world of observation. It may turn out that some of the implications of the false assumptions correspond quite accurately to real world observations. But that does nothing to establish the value of the instrument. The coincidence is only coincidence. To be useful, it would have to be known in advance *which* predictions could be relied upon. To show correspondence after the fact is merely to rationalize *post hoc.* A theory of motion developed for a planet where gravitational forces differed fundamentally from those found on earth might generate predictions that coincided perfectly with some aspects of the behavior of moving objects on earth. But they could not be considered predictions relating to earth and in advance of use they would certainly be rejected because of the known falsity of the premises. The reliability of predictors must be assessed before use; when premises are false, that is impossible.

Similar confusion sometimes arises with respect to the treatment of probabilistic propositions or statements in the form, "N percent of A is B." When such propositions are included in a theory, the results of calculation will necessarily be stated in percentages or probabilities. But the probabilistic character of the conclusions refers to their content and not to their logical status. Calculations used to deal with probabilistic statements are just as certain as any other. Their usefulness in social science is limited because the assumptions required for deductive reasoning are extremely hard to satisfy. For practical purposes, they can be used only for dealing with very large aggregates or very long sequences—a sample of the earth's atmosphere, for example, can be assumed to reflect the composition of the whole.

SOME PROBLEMS OF APPLICATION

It is useful to regard a theory as a device that isolates some set of observables completely from the rest of the environment and links their values by rule. In effect, it is assumed that the interrelations among those variables is so strong that the effect of changing the value of one variable can be determined completely within the set, given the rules. For the calculations to be made, isolation must be perfect. In the observed world, perfect isolation is never achieved, and if it were achieved, it would not be recognized. Some external factors always operate on any selected set of variables, though their influence may be relatively small. As the precision of measurement increases, the structure eventually becomes indeterminate.

No theory can be a perfect isomorph for observation, and it could not be demonstrated using human measurements. The deadlock is broken, and the logical requirements are satisfied, by *assuming* isomorphism, and using achievements made using the assumption to justify continuing to make it. The relation between consequences and purposes, in other words, justifies retaining the assumption of isomorphism needed to make calculation possible.

A practical and efficient way of dealing with external influences on the elements in a theory is to attach a Fudge Factor to the structure, placing it between theory and environment. All of the external influences that operate on the variables in the theory can be lumped together in the Fudge Factor. The extent of their combined influence can be determined by measuring the reliability of the structure; the elements involved need not be identified. If more reliability is needed, some of the influences contained in the Fudge Factor must be identified, and their influence specified and incorporated into the theory or the statement of limiting conditions. The Fudge Factor contains an unanalyzed collection of influences that can be summed collectively even if they have not been identified. The device greatly facilitates the task of applying theory since isomorphism can be produced by increasing the influence of the Fudge Factor without losing the essential calculability on which the process depends.

A special problem is created when a theory incorporates a set of variables that interact consecutively, producing the condition known as feedback between the variables. When that occurs, logic limits the size of the structure that can be created. The very large collections of variables produced by computer projections do not constitute *a* theory, even if causal relations have been established. They are a congeries of individual theories, physically juxtaposed but not integrated into a functioning whole. Theories that deal with feedback situations will usually consist of two or three active variables and a complex "ground" of limiting conditions. The reason is formal and apparently immutable. If there are five or more elements in a feedback structure, calculation is impossible in principle; if there are four, calculation is a practical impossibility.

The Fudge Factor provides a badly needed margin of error in weak disciplines such as the social sciences; it is also very useful for the policymaker. Without altering the cognitive status of the discipline, the device allows for development and use of weak, crude, and relatively unreliable theories as a basis for action when purposes are known and minimum reliability can be accepted. That approach to theorizing is not unique but commonplace. It is usually understood that powerful, sophisticated theories are very difficult to produce in social science; it is less commonly appreciated that such theories are also very difficult to create in physical science. Further, in the pragmatic terms appropriate for policymaking, theoretical adequacy is far more important than sophistication or even accuracy. Some use can be found for almost any theory that deals with significant phenomena, however weak it may be. A treatment for cancer that was effective in only 5 percent of all cases might be warmly welcomed if no better alternative could be found. Any potential causal relation can serve as a point of departure for efforts to control events. Needlessly severe formal requirements endanger the theoretical enterprise unjustifiably.

What emerges from a consideration of such aspects of theory development is the need to focus on useful instruments, however weak. A corollary requirement, however, is a serious commitment to maintaining the conditions of corrigibility in ongoing inquiry and in application. Weak theories are acceptable if they are taken as launch points for further improvements. The effort to control must remain firmly wedded to systematic efforts to improve. A minimum level of control may be acceptable for lack of something better, but should not be considered satisfactory. And efforts to improve without reference to the capacity to control are bound to be fruitless, for there would be no way to judge that an improvement had been made. Seeking both to control and to improve the capacity to control can make both efforts fruitful.

CRITICIZING AND TESTING THEORIES

Theories are here identified as instruments that make possible control over events in the environment. Such instruments cannot be evaluated by reference to general criteria alone. Justifications and criticism will always refer to experience. For the policymaker seeking instruments that can be used in his work, four aspects of theory are particularly important for evaluation: the adequacy of the theory for the purpose in hand; the internal characteristics of the structure; the degree of congruence with established knowledge;

and the evidence obtained over time from testing and application. Whether or not a theory is accepted, or retained, depends on the urgency of the need to act and the quality of the available alternatives. The perspective best suited to criticism in such cases is that of the surgeon who must decide whether or not to use new techniques of uncertain quality in his practice.

For the policymaker, theoretical adequacy is crucial. Some valuable insights into the meaning of adequacy as applied to theories is obtained by extending the analogy from theory to maps. Maps are descriptive and not generalized, and they record an incomplete selection of observations. The selection depends on the purpose. Maps can be developed that will serve more than one purpose but no map can serve all possible map users with equal efficiency. So it is with theories. The instrument must provide the required level of control over the proper events with acceptable reliability. Otherwise, richness and accuracy are irrelevant. The most difficult question is the level of reliability that can be expected in use, particularly if the theory is new or weak and experience with application is limited.

The internal characteristics of a theory are a matter for visual inspection. They include such points as the clarity and precision of the concepts employed, the general form in which the assumptions are stated, the indicators and the measurements employed, and so on. Of course, if the instrument is not meant to fulfill a specific purpose, and the population that will be used as a basis for evaluating the results of action cannot be specified, the rationale for such preliminary criticism is missing. Structurally, the rules incorporated into the theory must link all of the variables into an unbroken chain or network; the statement of limiting conditions must be rich enough to satisfy the observer with firsthand knowledge of the events to which the theory refers. The transformation rules should link the symbols firmly to specific observables. Theoretical terms, whose meaning can be determined only within the theory, may be included but the whole theory cannot consist in such terms—there must be some link to observation, or some basis for testing. Any assumption that differs significantly from accepted knowledge in the field should be specified and noted. And finally, the theory should be accessible to and testable by any adequately trained individual. The theory cannot be restricted in unusual ways that rule out use by competent specialists.

For any instrument to be used in making policies, the need to establish a causal relation among the variables in the set is crucial. Evidence of correlation is positive but inadequate. Both theories and forecasts are supported by evidence of correlation; the problem is to distinguish between the two. At a minimum, there must be some evidence to show that the theoretical structure functions as expected when acted upon, that it can be acted upon reliably and not merely used to predict the flow of natural events. The evidence may come from natural history or from deliberately contrived experiments. The source of evidence will influence evaluation to some degree, for the errors associated with each source are different. Evidence may even be indirect, through another established theory, so long as testing in action is not omitted completely.

It is worth noting that the role of experiments in scientific theorizing has often been much exaggerated, particularly in the mass media. The cinematic portrayal of a group of scientists breathlessly awaiting the outcome of a crucial test or experiment, though less prevalent today than a few decades ago, still persists. In most of the well-developed sciences, experiments tend to corroborate expectations, to test assumptions already firmly held, and not to generate startling new insights or information. In the early stages of development of a field, deliberate efforts to learn "What happens if. . ." may still be useful. Usually, the role of experiments is far less crucial for justifying assumptions or theories than might be supposed.

There is one important difference between theory testing in physical science and testing for theoretical adequacy in policymakng. In physical science, compatibility with existing knowledge is perhaps the most important test of proposed new theories. If the theory demands technology beyond present capacity, experimental testing will not be possible in any case. Lack of experimental evidence is not a serious handicap in such cases. But when theories are to be used in policymaking, a theory that cannot be implemented is useless. And in social science, the available supply of established theories is extremely small and testing against accepted theory is rarely adequate justification for use in everyday affairs. Those seeking theories that can serve as a base for action are in such cases well advised to ignore the elegance or parsimony of the theoretical formulation, or even the degree of fit between a particular theory and the body of accepted knowledge in the field, and insist on evidence of testing in action.[6]

In the social sciences, testing in use may also be difficult to carry out, and natural state evidence may not be reliable or accurate enough to serve as a test. In many cases, deliberate experimentation with human subjects is frowned upon, difficult to arrange, or even positively forbidden by society. In those circumstances, it seems the course of wisdom for social theorists to enter into much closer working relations with prospective users of their products, whether in government or in private business. Unfortunately, that is likely to require conditions that neither party is willing to accept. It would be extraordinarily difficult for a young economist to take the time and effort needed to become sufficiently familiar with organizational operations to be able to provide useful advice. For all practical purposes, that relationship would be equivalent to being fully employed by the organization. On the other hand, the management is unlikely to agree to the level of access to information, and the independence of judgment, that working theorists require since the implied risk of serious criticism is higher than most public or private bureaucrats willingly accept.

For social scientists, the available historical records are potentially a rich source of both theoretical relations and tests of those relations. In general, history registers events of interest to social rather than physical scientists. In a limited sense, history is the basic laboratory of the social sciences. It is somewhat surprising to learn how little it is used. Economists rarely refer to the work of economic historians. Of course, the data found in history are less precise and more selective than most social scientists would like, and omissions can be vexing. But the record of real world relations, including the link between action and consequence at many different scales or levels, has great potential value. Social science training apparently does not prepare the student to use that resource effectively. In an era that seems at times determined to substitute technical skill for familiarity with past human experience, it may be worth while to stress once again the role that history can and should play in the intellectual enterprise. All things considered, the history of real events is a far better guide, even for highly speculative inquiries, than either the results of laboratory experiments or estimates generated from assumptions of uncertain validity.

Probably the best test of a theory intended for policymaking is to make policy with it. Laboratory data are unsatisfactory because the aim of the policymaker is to function effectively in real world situations and not in isolation from real world constraints and influences. Genuine applications or natural state experiments are the ultimate test of theory. They require the capacity to make an accurate description of initial conditions so that the effects of action can be measured, and some ability to stabilize external influences, or at least incorporate them into the limiting conditions that control application of the theory. Here formal laboratories are useful, particularly for separating complex and delicate structures into their constituent elements or breaking apart the processes in sophisticated sequences of actions and interactions. For social science, however, real world affairs are the only locus where such external factors are present and sustained. Ultimately, theories must be isolated, captured, and brought under control in that domain.

Social science has been slow to experiment, either in the real world or in the laboratory. The technical difficulties associated with social experiments are not the principal reason for the tendency to shun experimentation. A major dissuading factor has been the antipathy with which human engineering is viewed by intellectuals and humanists, an antipathy much reinforced by some of the absurdities perpetrated by experimenters in psychology and elsewhere. Studies of human subjects that have as their only goal the satisfaction of an inquirer's curiosity, or his enrichment, are rightly condemned. But a clinical approach to experimenting, in which the aim is improvement of the conditions of life of the population involved, is another matter. There can hardly be serious objection to the physician's question if the medical assistance is needed and help is conditional on the information requested. It must be admitted that few social scientists, or educators, approach their work from that perspective, but it is clearly implied in a commitment to satisfying the requirements of reasoned policymaking, whether by the policymaker or by an external source.

When all of the testing and probing has been completed, in the laboratory or in the real world, no theory can be "proved" and no theory can be disproved. Such terms have meaning primarily in logic. Karl Popper demonstrated very convincingly the logical impossibility of positive proof of empirical propositions.[7] For empirical rather than logical reasons, disproof is equally beyond reach. All that can be done with theories is to weigh the evidence and the need and make a judgment, a not altogether satisfactory term for a very difficult task. Tomorrow's evidence may alter the judgment made today. Any theory is not necessarily better than no theory. It is reasonable for the drowning man to clutch at straws, but to look for straws when heavy logs are floating past on the floodwaters is a serious mistake in judgment or strategy.


## NOTES

1. There are two major differences between the approach to theory taken here and the conception used in most of classic philosophy of science. First, the requirement that a causal relation be assumed between the variables in a theory, which flows from the need to provide an instrument that can serve as a basis for action, is not generally found there; second, more emphasis is placed here on limiting conditions than in most of philosophy of science. Karl R. Popper, in *The Logic of Scientific Discovery* (Science Editions, 1961), Chapter 1 is required to take "cause" more seriously than most because of the emphasis placed on testability. Stephen Toulmin, in his *Philosophy of Science: An Introduction* (Harper and Row, 1960) asserts that interest in causes is confined to cases where people are "trying to get somewhere," and they are separated from the body of what he calls science in a curious way: "the term 'cause' is at home in the diagnostic and applied sciences, such as medicine and engineering, rather than in the physical sciences. For the theories of the physical sciences differ from those in the diagnostic and applied sciences much as maps differ from itineraries" (p. 121). In that context, what is offered here is a "philosophy of engineering." The standard definition of theory is approximately as follows: "a systematically related set of statements, including some lawlike generalizations, that is empirically testable." Richard S. Rudner, *Philosophy of Social Science* (Prentice-Hall, 1966), p. 10. See also Carl G. Hempel, *Aspects of Scientific Explanation* (Free Press, 1965); Ernest Nagel, *The Structure of Science* (Harcourt, Brace and World, 1961); or Richard B. Braithwaite, *Scientific Explanation* (Harper and Brothers, 1960). Differences in the approach to theory vary only in detail.

2. The best treatment of the topic remains Robert Bierstedt's "Nominal and Real Definitions in Sociological Theory," reprinted in *Symposium on Sociological Theory,* ed. Llewellyn Gross (Harper and Brothers, 1959), pp. 121-43.

3. Ibid., pp. 126-27.

4. A. S. Guha, "Neutrality, Monotonicity, and the Right of Veto," *Econometrica* 4, no. 5 (September 1972): 824.

5. William Ascher, *Forecasting: An Appraisal for Policy-makers and*

*Planners* (Johns Hopkins Press, 1978) provides some valuable insights into the process.

6. Henry Margenau, "What is a Theory?" in *The Structure of Economic Science: Essays on Methodology,* ed. Sherman R. Krupp (Prentice-Hall, 1966), pp. 32-33, uses such terms with respect to theory, but the example is rare.

7. Popper, *Logic of Scientific Discovery,* ch. 1.

# Economics and Policymaking

The essential features of the critical apparatus that will be used to assess the contribution of economics to policymaking have now been developed and their implications for inquiry briefly sketched. The starting point was the everyday conception of policy as a guide to action, an intellectual tool useful for satisfying significant human needs or purposes in the environment. The meaning of policy was refined and elaborated, and the structures, processes, and criteria required for reasoned policymaking were identified, within the framework provided by a theory of knowledge. That theory departs from conventional epistemology by focusing on the instruments and processes that can be used to improve the human situation through reasoned action, justified and improved out of experience over time. In that context, policies are rules of action that apply priorities or preferences to actions or choices. For critical purposes, the network of structures and processes involved in making defensible and corrigible policies must be taken as a whole. If policies are to serve as guides to action, then economists seeking to contribute to policymaking must provide some part of the knowledge on which reasoned action or choice depends. Their contribution must be measured against those requirements. Granting that policy can be examined from other perspectives, the necessary conditions for policymaking identified within any sound theory must be honored in all others. That is, various theories may suggest ways of changing the state of water from liquid to ice, but if a temperature below 32° F. is established as a necessary condition for that change, every proposed way of making ice must satisfy that limit or be expected to fail.

When the goal is defensible and corrigible policies useful for dealing with significant real world affairs, the instruments required of contributing disciplines are complex and the criteria of adequacy difficult to satisfy, particularly in social science. Policymaking demands both empirical and normative knowledge; each policy is in effect an experiment in improving the human condition by exercising reasoned control over events according to some established set of priorities. The normative aspects of choice or action are absolutely contingent upon the quality of the empirical knowledge available; the adequacy of the empirical apparatus is in turn contingent upon normative requirements. Neither can ignore the other completely. Labels aside, the primary empirical requirement is for an instrument that can link action to consequences (thus providing a projection of the outcomes from which choices are made) and can suggest an intervention strategy (a way of producing that preferred outcome). The requirement is satisfied by an instrument consisting of a selection of variables, a set of rules linking their values, a statement of limiting conditions, and an assumed causal relation among the elements. If the pattern is structurally and dynamically isomorphic to observation, calculations performed within the logic can be transferred to the observed world where they provide expectations and means for controlling events. Control in principle is not sufficient; the pattern must actually work. To contribute to reasoned policymaking, economics must produce such instruments, however they may be labeled.

A comparison of the products of economics and the requirements for reasoned policymaking supplies evidence of adequacy but cannot suggest ways of improving performance. For that purpose, the critic must return to the analytic framework, seeking not just the final product required for making policy but the constituent elements of structure and process that affect its quality.

A good analog is found in the way that a competent piano teacher improves student performance. To be competent, the teacher must derive from training and experience ways of relating particular aspects of playing to the quality of the final product, and learn to associate specific flaws in performance with corrigible inadequacies or errors. Criticism begins with the music coming from the piano but the analysis is carried out in terms of the factors that influence quality—phrasing, dynamics, rhythm, style, and various aspects of keyboard technique. The piece actually played is largely irrelevant if it demonstrates the critical dimensions of performance. To assess overall ability, enough of the repertoire must be heard to provide evidence on all of the major dimensions of the activity included in the critical framework. Within the teacher's conceptual-theoretical framework, that information provides grounds for judging the quality of the performance and for suggesting ways to improve it.

Doing economics, like playing the piano, involves an irreducible element of creativity and therefore cannot be formalized. But the theory of knowledge recommended here does suggest ways of increasing the likelihood of success in fulfilling the requirements of reasoned policymaking. Impediments to success can be recognized and eliminated; some strategies or lines of development are clearly more promising than others; omission of some considerations may seriously fault the inquiry. The theory of knowledge contains at least the rudiments of a theory of inquiry, and that structure can be used both to criticize and to suggest improvements in disciplinary performance.

The relation between economics and policymaking will be approached in that spirit and context. The primary concern is the adequacy of economic products for the policymaker's purposes: can economists supply the kind of instrument that the policymaker must have? Obviously, such instruments are most likely to be found among the theories that economists have produced. However, since much of economics is concerned with the creation of models of various kinds, there remains the possibility that some of those structures, however labeled, could actually satisfy the requirements for reasoned policymaking. Whatever the judgment eventually made, the basis for it must be articulated and related to recommended changes. That requires a critical framework, a theory of inquiry equivalent to the piano teacher's theory of play. The structure needed can be derived from the underlying theory of knowledge but it should be tested and refined in application. At present, only the bare rudiments of an adequate approach to inquiry can be identified with confidence, and they are offered tentatively. Nevertheless, they are already an invaluable base for both criticizing performance and suggesting ways of improving performance, *assuming that the purpose of inquiry is to contribute to reasoned policymaking.*

The products of contemporary economics will be evaluated for their contribution to policymaking along seven basic continua or dimensions. Each identifies one of the major prerequisites to successful performance in policymaking. Failure in any one of these areas means that the product cannot be used for reasoned policymaking, barring accident. Much of the work done in economics is deficient in several areas, however, and improvement in one may be inadequate. An adequate approach to inquiry should be able to satisfy the requirements along all seven continua, and more; these are necessary requirements and not sufficient conditions for success. There is some overlapping, and additional considerations could very easily be added. But criticism along these seven basic dimensions will bring out the major sources of inadequacy in economics and suggest some of the fundamental changes needed to correct them. They are equivalent to the principles used to criticize performance in pianists. The pianist who has not learned to pass the thumb under the fingers when playing scales, for example, cannot possibly play Liszt as it was written.

The selection of factors included in the critique was generated by examining the actual products of economics in terms of the necessary conditions for reasoned policymaking developed within the theory of knowledge. They pinpoint the primary reasons for product deficiency in the discipline, the areas where changes are needed before the policymaker's requirements can be satisfied and where changes could be expected to produce improved performance by economists. The same factors could be applied equally well to any other field of study. It is perhaps worth noting that most of the points of criticism are not new or unique; economists and others have criticized economics in these terms in the past. But the theoretical basis for criticism, or suggesting improvements, has not, to my knowledge, been articulated fully either within economics or in an allied field. Without a theoretical base, improved performance is very unlikely, if only because some theory is needed to identify an improvement and provide reasons for considering it an improvement. The continua refer to errors resulting from a fundamental misdirection of inquiry; such errors can only be corrected within a structure in which the policymaker's needs can be identified. Without a theoretical base, particular criticisms or suggestions could not be justified. Moreover, piecemeal improvements appended *ad hoc* could continue almost indefinitely without any significant advance in overall usefulness.

The seven aspects of economic inquiry primarily responsible for the observed inadequacies in research findings for policymaking are:

1. The purposes sought through inquiry
2. The procedures and strategies employed
3. The role played by description and observation, or data, in developing the body of economic knowledge
4. The kinds of instruments created
5. The assumptions incorporated into the theories and models
6. The tests applied to knowledge claims and the evidence offered to support them
7. The normative adequacy of the instruments created

An error in any one of these areas is usually sufficient to rule out use of the findings in reasoned policymaking.

## OVERVIEW: SEARCH AND FINDINGS

Because of the central role of theory in policymaking, and the relatively good fit between the meaning of *theory* in academic usage and its meaning in the more precise context of the theory of knowledge, the study began with an examination of general economic theory, broadly construed. As a performance pattern emerged and stabilized with respect to general economic theory, the inquiry was extended into other areas, including econometrics. So far as possible, both the leading journals and the work of outstanding practitioners were sampled, though less heavily than in theory. Some of the special branches of economics, notably agriculture, development, and international economics, were examined briefly, chiefly from the perspective of theories employed. A few issues of the leading European journals were included in the survey. The primary emphasis, however, is on American economic writings during the decade between 1970 and 1980. There is no way to determine the relative size of the sample, of course, but the consistency of the findings indicate that even a major extension of the sample would not produce very different results, whether in the United States or in Western Europe.

In most cases, books and articles couched entirely in formal terms or technical language were examined briefly and then set aside. That is the only avenue available for protesting against the practice, now widely condoned by editorial boards of learned journals, of allowing authors to state their purposes in the language of real world affairs and their reasoning and conclusions in the metalanguage used for analysis, generally some form of statistics. An example of the kind of material to which the objection specifically refers follows:

The utility interdependence hypothesis receives little support from my results. The estimated income elasticity for the primary dependent variable exceeds unity, as my model, augmented by the assumption that the consumption of others is a luxury, suggests. The coefficients of the variables used to represent the levels of consumption of potential recipients have the correct sign but . . .[1]

The author's judgment could be valid, and the dreadful "cannibal clause" in the second sentence could perhaps be ignored, but the intellectual effects of stating conclusions in the language of statistical analysis, as in the example, are most unfortunate—and justify halting the practice. For it is impossible to say whether or not the conclusions stated conflict with other knowledge of the phenomenon *until* a translation of meaning has been performed. Unless experience has been translated entirely into statistical terms (which is clearly impossible) or statistical statements are translated into real world terms, the practice objected to effectively rules out the use of real world experience in criticism.

There are, of course, good reasons for using technical languages. Indeed, all systematic criticism takes place within some metalanguage where purposes can be identified and the conditions to be fulfilled before the purpose is achieved can be stated. But there are equally good reasons for translating from technical language into the language of experience, and such translations are surely the responsibility of the author and not the reader. Only the author can say with assurance whether the precise meaning has been captured in a translation. The problems involved do not end there, however. If no translation is made, conclusions must be criticized solely by reference to the conventions that govern statistical usage. Those conventions are hardly well enough established to justify depending upon them when knowledge claims purport to refer to significant human affairs. In effect, the procedure tends to convert statistical analysis into a priestly language that excludes the uninitiated, or those unwilling to go through a tedious and too often unrewarding translation. Finally, it eliminates from inquiry the value added to the author's own knowledge by the process of translation, the effects of being forced to think about real world meanings, implications, and correspondence. All things considered, authors would do well to avoid the language of analysis for stating conclusions, and since authors tend to follow the path of least resistance to publication, editorial boards should certainly consider proscribing the practice.

Extending the scope of the study to include econometrics as well as economic theory and general economics produced surprisingly little change in the findings. For the most part, economic theorists and econometricians pursue the same goals with respect to the same overall phenomena using the same theoretical structures. Both focus on the economic system; both seek to develop formal logical structures that will explain and predict the operation of all or part of the economic system. The instruments produced are structurally identical, comprising sets of variables and rules of interaction linking their values. If the variables are features of the overall economic system, the inquiry is considered part of macroeconomics; variables that refer to the elements of the economic system fall within microeconomics. The distinction is not analytically useful, however, for there is as much diversity within each subdivision as between subdivisions. The branch of inquiry rather misleadingly labeled "welfare economics" is a part of macroeconomics that seeks reasons for preferring one state of the economic system to other system states. Most economists focus on the exchange of goods and services though some are concerned with production and distribution. Most deal with features of the economy, though some are concerned with the individual actor (producer, consumer, business manager, and so on) seeking to develop models of collective action based on assumptions that refer to the intentions or behavior of individuals.

The principal difference between economic theorizing and econometrics seems to lie in the role of real world data in the two enterprises. The econometrician usually begins with a body of historical data obtained from an official source and a set of theoretical assumptions taken from economic theory. The data are invariably aggregated, and may be ordered either into cross-sections or time series of varying densities. In many cases, the data are transposed into synthetic information, particularly in situations where direct observation is difficult or data are inaccessible. The goal of such inquiries, sought through formal modeling, is to explain or predict the historical data, using *explain* in the technical sense common in statistics and not in the sense in which it appears in contemporary philosophy of science. The rules and parameters incorporated into the model are estimated from the available data by various techniques, some very sophisticated.

The economic theorist usually begins with the existing body of economic theory rather than a body of data, with the set of assumptions currently employed to deal with some aspect of the economic system. The theorist is the keeper of the covenant in contemporary economics; the metaphor is quite accurate through a number of dimensions. Theorists most commonly extend, combine, integrate, or add to existing models or assumptions. Occasionally, a wholly new model or new set of assumptions is introduced and the implications of the structure explored. The theoretical enterprise in economics most closely resembles pure mathematics. It bears little resemblance to theorizing in the sciences, but it resembles superficially, and in a very misleading way, the work performed by theorists in physics.

Both the economic theorist and the econometrician will attend to those aspects of economic activity that attract attention in the real world—inflation, prices, unemployment, and so on. But if the track record established in the 1970s is maintained, neither is likely to approach such problems pragmatically, or with a sense of professional commitment to their solution. Theorists in particular deal with real world events by linking them to existing theories and generating "solutions" within those structures. The linkages are usually supplied through definitions rather than observations. At best, the criteria of success refer to improved predictability; more commonly, the solution remains untested. In a discipline richly supplied with sound theories, that procedure would be acceptable. But in a weak discipline it amounts to little more than changing the label on a bottle of patent medicine.

The principal finding of the study is unequivocal. *From the policymaker's perspective, both economic theory generally and econometrics are virtually useless. Their present products cannot be used in reasoned policymaking and their approach to inquiry makes future improvement extremely unlikely.* A competent policymaker will find little or nothing useful in the marketplace where the products of economics are displayed; that situation is unlikely to be different in the near future. The inadequacies of economics tend to be masked by the incompetence of policymakers, reinforced by the absence of competing alternatives—though it is possible that some public and private agencies have become self-reliant in these areas.

In effect, the theoretical capacity of economics has been grossly overrated, not least by economists themselves. Where policymaking is concerned, the implicit and often explicit assumption that economics is far more capable of providing needed theories than are the other social sciences is unwarranted. An examination of economic products suggests that economists are as much concerned with placing their wares in the academic shop windows as are members of other disciplines, and as little concerned with uses or applications. And the criteria that control access to the academic display system are unrelated to the usefulness of research findings in real world affairs. The evidence and justification for these conclusions will be summarized in the remainder of the chapter.

A very substantial part of the published material in economics can be discarded by the competent policymaker following cursory inspection. And the justification need not be perjorative. A surprisingly large number of economic publications bear no relation to real world affairs, and the authors make no claim to either theoretical validity or usefulness. For example, a great many articles in both econometrics and economic theory are merely technical studies, focused on the techniques used in analysis by those in the discipline. Such studies are easy to identify and they make no claim to contribute to policymaking. Again, studies which purportedly relate to real world affairs often state conclusions but do not claim they imply a course of action or solve any practical problems. The general rule, "What is not claimed need not be accorded" seems reasonable and appropriate in such cases. There are good reasons to assume that a valid claim to usefulness would be recognized and articulated, other things equal. Although usefulness is not rewarded positively within economics, there is no penalty attached to it either. Hence the absence of any claim is *prima facie* evidence against applicability. It remains possible that a particular study could have very extensive implications for the conduct of human affairs and not be recognized, but the materials found in the journals and other sources suggest that this rarely occurs.

Obviously, the converse of the rule does not hold. Claims to usefulness in policymaking do not warrant automatic acceptance or even serious consideration. In some cases, the form in which conclusions are stated make judgment difficult. It is relatively easy to reject purportedly useful studies whose conclusions assert that "our empirical results encourage us to believe that a disaggregate multivariate approach is useful for the study of fertility and labor supply behavior," or "this paper has shown how a theory of second best can be extended from the work of Baumol and Bradford to a case in which intermodal competition exists." Studies that are "useful for estimating," "better than other models," or "feasible for analyzing" an activity, generally fall into the same category. Stronger claims may require an examination of the whole report before they can be assessed. For example, the statement "I have argued that a stable price emerges as a result of the entrepreneur's attempt to manage endogenously generated uncertainties," could not be rejected until it was learned that the conclusion was generated from a set of postulates of uncertain quality and not from a systematic study of prices. Similarly, the claim that a paper can "explain the prevalence of several different insurance contracts observable in the real world," would attract the attention of policymakers until it was learned that the solution was sought through the same postulational procedures and without reference to data.[2] A quick examination of purpose, conclusion, evidence, and reasoning will usually lead to rejection of such efforts. The conclusions hold only within a set of assumptions whose relevance to real world affairs is uncertain, or even unlikely. Finally, there are published works that assert relevance to current problems, but only in principle—applicability is denied. Some claim that further study or additional information is required, with the suppressed implication that it is forthcoming. Others point to inadequacies in technology as the reason why testing or application are not presently possible. From the point of view of the policymaker, both claims mean that the results cannot be used.

When all such cases have been eliminated, only a very small part of total production in economics remains—between 5 and 10 percent of content of *The American Economic Review* for the period 1970-1980, on the most favorable rules of assessment possible and slightly more in some of the other journals. That number must be reduced further. When an economist claims that the feasibility and usefulness of a particular model or approach has been established, the implications of the claim will depend on particulars. The same uncertainty arises in econometrics when it is asserted that a model is able to predict historical data relating to a particular phenomenon. Many such inquiries merely demonstrate that a particular type of analysis can be made of a given body of data and do not show that the results of such analysis have value in policymaking.[3] An equally difficult claim to assess, which appears frequently in economic theory, is that a particular structure has great value for "understanding and predicting significant aspects of human behavior."[4] Given the vagueness of the term, claims to further "understanding" should probably be discounted almost entirely for it seems unrelated to any particular kind of performance. Claims to predictive capacity, taken by themselves, also leave the policymaker uncertain of the value of an instrument. If the instrument can do no more than predict, it can serve no useful purpose beyond pointing to the need for action. Prediction is a necessary but not a sufficient condition for reasoned policymaking. But many instruments useful for controlling events are also used as predictors, and economists as a whole do not make the distinction very often. The assessment of the instrument therefore remains incomplete until further evidence is obtained.

Further, the extent to which economic inquiry is "discipline-directed," acquires significance within the overall economic paradigm, or the particular conceptual-theoretical structure used in a subfield, introduces yet another complication into the assessment of quality. In the extreme case, as George Stigler observed, "whether a fact or development is significant [in economics] depends primarily on its relevance to current economic theory."[5] Assessing the value to policymaking of conclusions generated by such studies can be a very difficult matter. Consider three examples: "the goal of this paper is to embellish the theory of adjustment costs in a way that is consistent with observations about firm growth rates,"[6] "this conclusion has important implications for the theory of demand for money," and "the purpose of this paper was to reconcile the income-investment accelerator with the neoclassical theory of the competitive firm."[7] Careful examination showed that the implications of all three studies were confined strictly within economics and could be ignored by the policymaker, but the residue of uncertainty would be disturbing if each referred to humanly significant problems.

   The amount of economic theorizing and econometrics that makes an explicit claim to policy relevance is very small. Virtually all members of this class can also be rejected, but the reasons are more complex and the analysis must be more detailed and extensive. The central thrust of the argument against the various forms of economic theory, including the theories employed in econometrics, is that the activities, procedures, and criteria employed to create and validate them are unacceptable in a scientific enterprise. Theoretical inquiry in economics resembles mathematics rather than physical science. The phenomenon studied is the economic system, which is already an analytic structure and not an observable. The goal of inquiry is a formal model of the total system or one of its elements or features. The capacity of the model is usually unspecified; at most, the goal of "explaining and predicting" is borrowed from contemporary philosophy of science. Theoretical work ranges from extension, modification, or replacement of the axioms in an established structure to the creation of new sets of axioms and exploration of their implications. Unlike mathematicians, economists usually identify their symbols with concepts used for dealing with real world problems. But the transformation rules linking symbol to observation are rarely if ever provided and the isomorphism of system and observation remains untested. Most theoretical studies focus narrowly on the logical dimensions of formal models ignoring constraints, limitations in application, or adequacy of assumptions. References to events in the real world frequently, and perhaps nearly always, involve an improper transfer of a nominally defined term to the world of experience. When such procedures are used to generate policy suggestions, acceptance and use are not warranted. The cognitive status of economic theories is at best uncertain. To the question, How much credence should be attached to policy recommendations developed from contemporary economic theory? the weight of evidence clearly suggests the answer must be None!

The weaknesses in economic theory that justify such an adverse judgment are well known and frequently noted by economists, though the implication drawn here is usually avoided. George Stigler, for example, made precisely the same point in 1975:

The essential ambiguity of general theoretical systems with respect to public policy, however, has been the real basis of our troubles. So long as a competent economist can bend the existing theory to either side of most viable controversies without violating the rules of professional work, the voice of the economist must whisper in the legislative halls.[8]

But the assertion that economists have whispered in the legislative halls accords poorly with history, and they have assuredly roared in the media, usually providing a good illustration of Stigler's point by disagreeing volubly and pointedly about fundamentals.[9] Unfortunately, the implications of the current state of economic theory for use in policymaking are not usually drawn within economics, or elsewhere, nor are its causes identified.

Doubtless, some economists would be happy to sever all relations with everyday problems; some have already done so *de facto* if not *de jure*. But most economists seem unprepared to accept the role of intellectual and social eunuch willingly, publicly committing themselves and the profession to solipsistic pursuit of arcane activities at collective expense for purely selfish reasons. If nothing else, the willingness and even eagerness of economists to offer advice on matters of policy belies a lack of concern. There is genuine value, then, in identifying the sources of weakness that most hamper development of useful, justifiable, and corrigible economic theories, and

suggest changes likely to produce humanly useful production aimed
at significant goals. That is the point to which discussion now turns.

## THE SOURCES OF WEAKNESS

It cannot be emphasized too strongly that the principal source of
weakness in economics, the primary reason economics has not
developed products that can be used in policymaking, is found
in the set of assumptions that direct the enterprise, in the methodological and epistemological underpinning on which the discipline
depends, and the conception of inquiry that underpinning fosters
and supports. It would be pointless to calculate the percentage of
total publications examined in which particular errors appear, to
show that in n percent of all cases where policy advice was offered,
the instruments used to generate the advice contained no causal
assumption and therefore could not be used for that purpose. Such
instruments are *symptoms* of weakness and not its cause. The aim
here is to locate the underlying errors in the concept of inquiry and
show how they affect performance. That allows the individual to
test the analysis against unique cases, and it suggests remedies,
ways of improving the discipline's capacity to offer advice in policy
matters. If the analysis is sound, correcting particular symptoms
would have no more than a palliative effect.

Considering the reputation of the profession, the sophistication
of its mathematical apparatus, the volume of its products, and the
extent of its influence, the inadequacy of the epistemological-methodological foundation, and the limited awareness of such problems
within the discipline is truly astonishing. Economic theorizing in
particular emerges as a living anachronism, a curious throwback
to the age of rationalism. In some respects, it is actually presci-
entific, in the contemporary sense, rising at best to the level of
Newtonian physics and ignoring what has occurred since. The contrast with current conceptions of the scientific enterprise is both
striking and discouraging. The historical reasons for such miscon-
structions lie beyond my competence, though an early marriage
with Newtonian mechanics seems a likely explanation of current
practice. More recently, economics has taken its model of science
from theoretical physics rather than the more mundane experimental disciplines or the taxonomic natural sciences, and to a very

large extent its science has been learned from the philosophers of science rather than the scientists themselves—an outcome hard to avoid, in a way, because working scientists tend not to talk very much about the nature of science.

For any social science, emulation of theoretical physics is particularly unfortunate if only because the considerable temporal and conceptual distance that separates physics from even its modern origins tends to obscure some of the fundamentals. Theoretical physics can function today *because* the physics of a century ago, which was quite different and which still has parallels in most other fields within physics, produced the foundations on which the contemporary theoretical edifice is built. Theoretical physics is possible because there has been and continues to be an experimental physics; without it, the activity would soon become metaphysics and nothing more. Theories in physics, as in any other science, must remain grounded in observation. Theoretical peregrinations, however lofty, remain tied to the world of experience or lose their power to convince. Analytically, if no longer historically, inquiries in physics begin in the experienced world and they seek, ultimately, to bring the phenomena observed under control, to reproduce them, and perhaps use them in other areas. A relatively sharp division has been made between those who develop the theoretical apparatus (the pure scientists) and those who apply that apparatus to everyday affairs (the engineers). But the apparatus itself must be capable of controlling events, else it could not be used by engineers. And since the engineers often produce their own control apparatus, it becomes very difficult to separate the two tasks functionally or in any other useful and meaningful way, or to find a role for the pure theorist.

A number of preliminaries, analytically prior to theorizing, but wholly or partially suppressed in most treatments of the process need to be kept in mind as the discussion proceeds. The things to be studied must first be bounded, measured, and examined for attributes and relations, then organized into generalized frameworks. The profound taxonomic impulse in science is perhaps most readily seen in the early stages of historical development, or in some of the natural sciences. Without it, efforts to develop generalized instruments with even limited predictive capacity would be unlikely to succeed. The cumulated knowledge in well-established fields is perhaps the most important tool available for developing and testing still more knowledge. In systematic inquiry, as in economic activity, "Them that has, gets!" Remove what is known of the phenomena that concern the physicist, and that discipline very quickly rejoins economics and the remainder of the social sciences. There can be a division of labor in any field, of course, but the validity of dividing up the work depends on the status of the discipline as a whole, not the character of the division. To borrow procedures and practices from theoretical physicists without being able to borrow or create the other conditions that make them fruitful is to invite disaster, intellectually and economically.

Broadly construed, the scientific enterprise can serve as a valid frame of reference for all of the empirical disciplines. To the extent that the sources of strength in physical science can be identified and practices that would erode its capacity can be located and avoided, the physical sciences provide a useful model for emulation. But if the aim is to create a base for reasoned policymaking, the model of science must be applied and not pure. And within economics, if a distinction is to be made between those who are "pure" and those who "apply," and there is no evidence of such separation at present, then the applied branch of the discipline will still have to change its accepted approach to inquiry or remain sterile. If the discipline remains unified and retains its present approach to inquiry, then intellectual integrity surely requires economists to remain silent on matters of action or policy.

THE PURPOSE OF INQUIRY

There is no possibility of creating an intellectual basis for reasoned action that does not depend on human capacity to control the flow of real world events to some degree. Control over events depends in turn on the ability to link action to consequences accurately and reliably, through a calculable pattern, and assuming a causal connection or constant conjunction of events. A discipline that provides guidance in action must generate instruments that can satisfy those requirements and provide justification for the causal assumption they incorporate. Those requirements seriously constrain the purposes sought through inquiry and the way in which inquiry is conducted.

At present, the policymaker's need to control events virtually eliminates economics from policymaking. Very few of the economists studied sought deliberately, openly, and knowingly to gain control over real world events. At best, statements of purpose entailed that capacity only indirectly. In Kenneth Boulding's *Papers,* for example, the social scientist's principal task is stated in a form that hints at control and intervention. The task is "to reveal just where the alternatives lie, for mistakes in social policy arise more from lack of appreciation of the true alternatives involved than from deliberate mischoice."[10] Similarly, Wassily Leontief in a discussion of planning argues that the process should *not* start out with "the formulation of what theoretical economists refer to as the general 'objective function' but with elaboration of alternative scenarios each presenting in concrete, nontechnical terms one of the several possible future states of the economy."[11] By implication, at least, that would require the capacity to produce such states deliberately.

The exception is found among econometricians, where the use of models for making economic policy demonstrated very early the need to establish the causal relations that make control over events possible. Herman Wold's summary of the status of econometrics, published in 1969, is clear and decisive on the point:

In Tinbergen's models, and many other econometric models, the *ceteris paribus* assumption included rules of the game specified in terms of instruments and targets. This assumption is of a cause-effect nature.

The situation may be summarized as follows (and again I believe there is a more or less complete consensus about these points):

(i) The cause and effect specification of individual parameters of a forecasting model is formally in line with a stochastic specification of the relations in terms of predictors, and is a conceptually distinct additional hypothesis which may or may not be realistic and may or may not be adopted.

(ii) Causal specification . . . is not needed if none of the variables in the model is subject to manipulation or control. . . .

(iii) Causal specification is a necessity . . . if one or more of the variables in the model are subject to manipulation or control. . . .

(iv) Causal specification . . . is necessary if the future pattern of variability is foreseen to involve changes.[12]

The need for causal specification is clear and the reasons compelling. In fact, very few of the econometric models examined contained a causal assumption. Presumably at least, the difficulty lies in the development of adequate criteria of causality that can be tested statistically, that is, statistical procedures for demonstrating causality.[13]

Econometrics aside, economists who make statements about the purposes of inquiry most commonly opt for prediction as the basic aim. In Milton Friedman's famous essay on methodology, for example, the "ultimate goal of positive science" is to develop a "theory" or "hypothesis" that "yields valid and meaningful . . . predictions about phenomena not yet observed." James Buchanan, discussing the purposes of positive economics from a different perspective, focused on "attempting to understand a certain type of human behavior and the prediction of the social structures that are emergent from that behavior."[14] Where economists have made contact with philosophy of science, the need to "explain events in the real world and make correct predictions" is the most common statement of purposes, though "understanding" is sometimes substituted for "explaining." The term remains undefined in both cases. Occasionally, the need to focus on explaining and predicting is reinforced by specifically excluding "control" over events from the purposes of scientific inquiry:

Now, if the layman is chiefly concerned with the power of science to control events, the scientist is rather concerned with its power to explain and predict correctly, for the power to control events is a byproduct of successful explanation. . . .[The power to control] is, however, itself neither an aspect of science nor a methodological standard by which to judge it. A hypothesis is verified by using it to make predictions.[15]

By leaving the meaning of "explain" unclear, that position can be made to sound plausible. But if an adequate explanation *can* provide control over events, then the instrument that provides the explanation must have the attributes required of an instrument that can control events in the environment. In that case, differences in labeling are unimportant. If, however, an adequate explanation could be provided *without* providing the capacity to control events, and that is certainly possible given the normal use of explanation in philosophy of science, then Grunberg's account is inaccurate and misleading.

The most suggestive approach to the problem of controlling events, and the treatment of causality it requires, is found among the economic conservatives. F. A. Hayek, for example, in the 1974 Nobel lecture entitled "The Pretence of Knowledge," flatly denied that human efforts to control events could succeed, and made it clear that such an outcome was in any case undesirable. Stressing the "insuperable limits" to human knowledge, Hayek very strongly attacked what he called "man's fatal striving to control society." The grounds for the opposition are essentially ideological and normative. The ability to control events carries with it the power to coerce, and ". . . even if such power is not in itself bad, its exercise is likely to impede the functioning of those spontaneously ordered forces by which, without understanding them, man is in the real world so largely assisted in the pursuit of his aims."[16] Hayek's position is extreme, and easy to distinguish, but precisely the same attitude is implicit in the more common distinction between science and engineering. For example, R. A. Gordon's presidential address to the American Economic Association contained a strong criticism of the excessive emphasis on logical rigor current in economics and the corresponding loss of relevance to everyday affairs. Gordon went on to say that economics had been most successful when rigorous formulations of theory had been relaxed. He did not conclude, as might be expected, that economics should therefore move closer to engineering, noting instead that those parts of economics that had followed this route to relevance ". . . resemble more a branch of engineering rather than a social science," implying that this was *not* economics as science and that he was unprepared to follow the same path.[17]

Although the difference between seeking accurate predictions, or even predictions and explanations, rather than the capacity to control events may seem minor, it serves as a fundamental demarcation line for policymaking inquiries. A discipline based on prediction can issue early warning signs but has no way of evading or modifying expectations. The situation in seismology illustrates the position. The economic system must be treated as a natural phenomenon like the solar system; it can be studied and charted but not changed. The result of rigorous adherence to that approach would be science without engineering. There is a substantial difference between demanding no more than prediction and asserting that no more is possible in principle. But the practical effect is precisely the same in both cases, and the effect on the approach to inquiry is disastrous if the goal is policymaking. In that context, a discipline that accepts prediction as the primary goal of inquiry serves the same function for the conservative economist that gun control legislation serves for the political radical, though less obviously. In both cases, fear of abuse leads to efforts to eliminate the instrument whose abuse is feared; and in both cases, the fear is so great that side effects of fear tend to be ignored.

BASIC PROCEDURES AND STRATEGIES

One of the few points on which general agreement can be had among contemporary philosophers of inquiry is that there can be no "scientific method" that need only be rigorously enforced to produce valid and valuable knowledge. Any set of assumptions that can survive all available means of testing knowledge claims is considered acceptable regardless of author or mode of production. That much said, if the function of systematic inquiry is to organize human experience to purpose, and more specifically, to achieve control over the environment, as it must for reasoned policymaking, some procedures are much more likely than others to produce viable results. In particular, it seems clear that experience is prior to organization, and that enormous theoretical leaps are less likely to be successful, particularly in the early stages of inquiry, than small increments.

The historical development of the physical sciences strongly supports reliance on experience as a base. Indeed, they were at one time referred to as the "inductive" sciences to acknowledge the basic procedure used to acquire and expand knowledge. Unfortunately, that term has been heavily contaminated by the ongoing controversy over inductivism in the style of Sir Francis Bacon. His famous *hypotheses non fingo* ("I do not frame hypotheses"), suggested that science observed, recorded, and somehow simply transformed factual statements into scientific knowledge.[18] In contemporary science and philosophy of science, it is more or less taken for granted that science proceeds by formulating and testing hypotheses or assumptions about the phenomena observed. That is not, however, inconsistent with the view that observation is analytically prior to generalization, in most if not all cases, and that science proceeds inductively, in the sense that theory is created by generalizing experience and the latter comes first both analytically and historically.

Construed in that less restrictive sense, induction contrasts sharply with the postulational or rationalist approach to inquiry that characterizes much of economics, and economic theory in particular. The essential features of the postulational process are more readily seen in basic texts, or in transfers of economic strategy and procedure to other fields, than in sophisticated theoretical works. In the latter, the nature of the original postulations is usually masked by several layers of derivation and borrowing. But in basic texts, the character of the underlying model is usually articulated more clearly. Thus McKenzie and Tullock begin with the choosing or decisionmaking individual and develop a set of assumptions that underlie all of the subsequent analysis.

First, in economics the individual is assumed to be ''rational'' in the sense that he is able to determine within limits what he wants and will strive to fulfill as many of his wants as possible.

. . . the individual will always choose more of what he wants rather than less.

. . . if there is uncertainty surrounding the available bundles, the individual will choose that bundle for which the *expected value* is greatest.

He will never obtain a perfect world; and as a result, he must accept second best, which is to maximize his utility through his behavior.

The assumption that the rational individual maximizes his utility implies that he will fully allocate his income among those things he wants.

The assumption also implies that the individual will continue to consume a given good until the marginal cost of the last unit obtained is equal to the marginal utility.[19]

Only a partial selection of the assumptions is reproduced, but it should clarify their basic character.

Now, McKenzie and Tullock know perfectly well that the assumptions specify a mode of behavior that is in some respects beyond human capacity, "No individual is really able to act in as precise a manner as the above discussion may imply." But the significant point in a theory is whether humans actually *do* act in this way. Are the assumptions generalized from observations of past behavior, or merely postulated? In fact they are only postulates, and the strongest evidence for the prevalence of the procedure is the degree of unreality incorporated into the assumptions that economists use, a point examined in detail below. The kind of reasoning involved is best seen in an example, this time taken from an application of economics to politics. Noting that "economic theory has been erected upon the supposition that conscious rationality prevails," Anthony Downs goes on to identify the characteristics of a rational actor more specifically, though along parallel lines:

Economic rationality can also be formally defined in another manner. A rational man is one who behaves as follows: (1) he can always make a decision when confronted with a range of alternatives; (2) he ranks all the alternatives . . . (3) his preference ranking is transitive; (4) he always chooses . . . that which ranks highest . . . and (5) he always makes the same decision each time he is confronted with the same alternatives.[20]

Like McKenzie and Tullock, Downs has no illusions about the character of the assumptions, and calls attention to the discrepancy between assumptions and observation, "Empirical studies are almost unanimous in their conclusion that adjustment in primary groups is far more crucial to nearly every individual than more remote considerations of economic or political welfare." If the assumptions were construed as generalized experience in the loose inductive sense that would be the end of the matter, for they would not be tenable. But the economist, and those who accept the economic approach to inquiry, can proceed undeterred: "Nevertheless, we must assume men orient their behavior chiefly toward [economic or political welfare] in our world; otherwise, all analysis of either economics or politics turns into a mere adjunct of primary-group sociology."[21] There could be no clearer example of the kind of unwarranted and unacceptable actions that a commitment to inductive procedure avoids.

Technically, reliance upon postulation rather than generalization from observation and experience reduces the set of concepts used in analysis to symbols nominally defined, with all of the limitations that implies. The logical structure can be clarified, but the meaning of terms ("rational actor," for example) cannot be challenged on empirical grounds. The price of such freedom of action is irrelevance with respect to real world affairs. And common acceptance of postulation as a legitimate procedure, particularly within economic theory, means that all of the products of that subdiscipline can, and indeed must, be regarded with considerable suspicion by those seeking tools to be used as a basis for real world action. The postulational approach to theorizing has extensive implications for other aspects of inquiry, and the effect is usually to compound inadequacies rather than remove them. Accordingly, an economics oriented to the production of useful instruments for policymaking would at least have to modify the criteria applied to the assumptions incorporated into its theories.

DATA: THE ROLE OF OBSERVATION AND DESCRIPTION

In the physical sciences, observation, description, and taxonomy have played a key role in inquiry from the beginning of the modern period. In consequence, most physical sciences are data-rich and more information is constantly being produced. Indeed, the wealth of data actually allows development of special branches of theory that can function in an almost wholly abstract atmosphere without losing touch with reality. The situation in economics is radically different. Economists produce little evidence themselves; observation, description, and taxonomy play almost no role in general economics. Indeed, there are remarkably few taxonomies available in the discipline, which is an indication of the extent to which it depends on nominally defined terms in its theorizing. Further, descriptive data are not extensively used for developing and testing theory. In a casual selection of 8 volumes of the *American Economic Review* published between 1978 and 1980, there were exactly 100 major articles. Of these, fully two-thirds contained no data, and referred to no data, either to support an argument or to indicate the experience from which theory had been generalized. Surprisingly, in a parallel selection of issues of *Econometrica,* containing 156 major articles, there were 78 that contained no data. And the data that are used by economists are almost invariably aggregated and in many cases synthesized or reduced to index numbers. Most of the data in use were supplied by public authority; most were developed for a purpose different from that of the article or according to some standard formula. Occasionally, evidence obtained by survey is cited but direct descriptive accounts are rare.

The primary role of observation in science hardly needs argument, though that does not imply support for the extreme inductivism that Bacon favored. Scientists must both abstract from observation (omit details, aggregate, and integrate) and generalize observations (create propositions not limited in time and place that serve as storehouses for information). Observation provides the statement of initial conditions needed as evidence of change, and the sequences of descriptive accounts needed to test assumptions about change or the actions that produce it. The absence of an adequate and accurate descriptive base literally guarantees against the development of useful and acceptable instruments for controlling events in the environment, in economics as in any other discipline. That inadequacy has often been noted, of course, but there is no evidence within economics of systematic efforts to improve. Economic historians sometimes record extensive and accurate descriptions of events. But economic theorists and econometricians rarely cite economic history, and economic historians do not refer frequently to the work of theorists, which may account for some of the discrepancies between production and use. The end result, whatever the cause, is the situation described by Wassily Leontief, "the weak and all too slowly growing empirical foundation clearly cannot support the proliferating superstructure of pure, or should I say speculative, economic theory."[22] The criticism is just, and in fact too moderate. General economics, and economic theory in particular, appears precisely analogous to a vast area of brush and scrub timber with only the barest rudiments of a root system. What is surprising, given the weakness of the descriptive foundations and the extreme vulnerability of the structure to systematic criticism, is how such theories have managed to remain standing for so long when they use symbols that refer to real world events. Delphic pronouncements, and references to complex structures whose elements, combined with failure to specify time limits, seem to account for survival, but it would be useful to know more of the process.

One major reason for the present descriptive weakness of economics is the disciplinary focus on "the economic system" and its various elements or features. The primary object of inquiry is only an analytic structure, a second order concept or construct, and not an observable. For some purposes, that focus has great advantages. Analytic systems are easily bounded and broken into constituent elements; system states can be identified or postulated. The interaction of the elements can be dealt with holistically, as with the solar system, and that is very attractive to national policymakers. The price of analytic clarity, however, is the great difficulty that economists encounter when they try to relate their findings to real world affairs. And it is not very easy to see how an individual observer could be most effectively positioned in the economic system, given the abstract character of economic concerns. It is hardly surprising that observation and description has been increasingly subordinated to speculation and postulation within the discipline. And as familiarity and practice produces further abstraction of the original construct, creating reality control becomes an even more serious problem. Moreover, the readiness with which analytic systems are bounded can be very misleading, for in real society, separation of the empirical dimensions of everyday life from the rest is impossible to achieve precisely. The effects of action within the "economic" sector always spill over into other aspects of social life. If the analytic framework employed in the study of economics blocks out such side effects, an important part of the costs and benefits of economic actions can be ignored, creating the kind of normative inadequacy in policymaking to be discussed later.

From another perspective, if the analytic structure is put together from observation and generalization, or created inductively and not through postulation, the concepts employed will have real definitions and testable or challengeable empirical meanings. Indeed, such concepts would usually incorporate the taxonomies created out of the initial effort to order and arrange experience with the phenomena being studied. Instead, most of the basic terms used in economics are defined nominally; there are very few genuine concepts or classifications, terms whose meanings can be disputed on empirical grounds in the same way as mumps or groundhogs. No one can say with respect to such terms as supply, demand, market, competition, or monopoly, that the meaning offered for the term does not correspond to observations of the phenomenon, in the same way that a definition of mumps or groundhogs can be challenged. The applicability of the concept can be questioned but not the meaning. Economic *terms* (for they are not, strictly speaking, concepts in the usual sense) tend to have *no* real world meaning; their meaning is contained completely in their formal definitions.

That causes no problems so long as separation from real world affairs is maintained. But the terms used in economics are treated as genuine *concepts,* and they are firmly established in everyday usage, and that creates the illusion (sic) that economists discuss real world problems in their professional work. And since some economists certainly do just that, and all make use of roughly the same professional vocabulary, that further complicates the tangle of limits on usefulness.

An illustration will suggest the depths of the conceptual confusion, and the difficulties involved in assessing the cognitive status of conclusions advanced by economists on the basis of their theorizing.

Assume that separate owners of cattle share grazing rights to *common* territory. Land is commonly owned and all cattle owners have grazing rights. In this situation, each cattle owner may have a private incentive to overgraze the common land.

An institutional reform that would surely eliminate the overgrazing on the land is the granting of private ownership rights to land, to convert commonly owned property into private property. Once this step is taken, the private owners of the land have an incentive to restrict the usage of the resource to socially optimal levels.[23]

That innocuous, and seemingly reasonable suggestion in fact results from a wholly illegitimate transfer from a formal model to the real world, coupled with a gross logical fallacy.

The first paragraph can be granted without quarrel. There *may* be an incentive for the individual to overgraze collectively owned land. But the second paragraph begins with a "complex question" fallacy, assuming that overgrazing *has* occurred, though that is neither logically necessary nor empirically established by the argument. The conclusion, that institution of individual property rights will "surely" eliminate overgrazing is at best a *non sequitur.* It would follow in a model which assumed a rational actor and circumstances that did not require overgrazing. And an incentive to restrict produces restriction with certainty only in a formalized calculus. In the real world, private ownership of inadequate land may still lead to overgrazing simply to extend survival even though the overgrazing may in the long run reduce the probability of survival, a double bind that is all too common in the less-developed nations. And the "socially optimal" level of grazing expected from conversion to private ownership is only a matter of definition: *any* outcome produced under stipulated conditions within the model will be "socially optimal," for that is all that is meant by the term. The recommendations literally have no force in real world affairs. Yet the illusion of argument is created, and people, including policymakers, are often deceived by it.

Lest the focus of criticism be misread, let me emphasize that the objections made do not refer to the use of *some* nominally defined or theoretical terms in systematic inquiry. Every theory in science incorporates some terms whose meaning depends entirely on the theoretical context. But no genuine theory in science, and no instrument useful for controlling the environment, can be constructed *entirely* of theoretical terms or nominally defined symbols. Some parts of the structure must consist in genuine concepts, terms whose meaning is rooted in observation. The physical sciences satisfy those requirements almost casually, though in the outer reaches of theoretical physics the relation to evidence may be tenuous and difficult to establish. Economics, like the other social sciences, is very far removed indeed from that level of theoretical activity.

From a slightly different perspective, the life history of the concepts and terms used in economics suggests yet another consequence of the failure to ground the discipline adequately in observation. Ordinarily, nominally defined terms are introduced into scientific inquiry to provide a needed link in an established structure of relations. In due course, the term becomes a concept, or a theoretical term whose meaning is adequately defined within the context of the theory. The same type of evolution occurs in applied sciences such as medicine, or rocketry. Among the self-proclaimed sciences, economics has a truly unique conceptual history. For the same set of nominally defined terms have been in use almost from the inception of the discipline without either significant modification or serious test of utility. Again, the reason that situation has been allowed to continue seems related to the analytic construct used as a focus of inquiry, or the distance that separates theory and observation.

One additional characteristic of contemporary economics that should perhaps be attributed to the absence of a close relation between theory and observation is the widespread use of concepts that are exceptionally difficult to operationalize, that is, to link to specific indicators and measurements. A mathematical specification of the meaning of *equilibrium* may not be particularly difficult, for example, but what kinds of indicators could be used to show that an economic system had actually reached that state? or to decide an economy was moving toward it or away from it? Pareto optimality, which is the cornerstone of welfare economics, is defined as a situation in which no one could be made better off without making someone else worse off. Ignoring the problems associated with such terms as better and worse, what criteria could be used to identify the condition in real life? More importantly, what indicators would show that society was approaching or departing from a Pareto optimal state? Logically, "a step in the right direction" cannot be identified until the complete course has been charted, common usage notwithstanding. But if Pareto optimality could not be recognized when reached, then a step toward or away from that state would also be unrecognizable. How, then, can the concept be used in real world affairs? And if the concept has no applicability, what is gained by developing a formal apparatus that depends upon it?

The overall effect of such practices is to make the economist, and not just the economic theorist, a traveler from another world in which the rules of behavior and interaction are all different. Inquiry then becomes a game consisting of statements in the form, "If the world were like this, things would behave in the following manner." If an imaginary world can be created that approximates the perceived world in known though limited ways, which is all that can be asked of any forecast or theory, calculations within that imaginary world can be meaningful and useful, as in Kenneth Boulding's treatment of "images." If the two worlds are very disparate, if the rules differ markedly, then manipulation of the imaginary structure is merely a logical exercise, a shuffling of words and symbols and not an effort to organize experience through a hypothetical pattern.

INSTRUMENTS

For reasoned policymaking, an instrument is needed that can direct human action to the achievement of a preferred outcome, that serves to control the flow of events. To provide such an action base, a causal assumption must link a set of rule-connected variables.

Nomenclature varies, but contributions to policymaking must be capable of the required functions however they may be labeled. In general, adequate instruments are most likely to be found among the structures labeled theories, but the availability of theories does not guarantee that adequate instruments are available and some may be found in other products of inquiry.

Economics generates a great many potential instruments. Perhaps 80 percent of the published works examined contained some kind of model or logical structure. Unfortunately, most turned out to be Dr. Seuss machines, logics without applications. They could be manipulated but not applied. The status of the remainder is uncertain but dubious. Economists rarely search for ways of controlling events nor do they claim to be able to control events through their theories. Moreover, testing in use against pragmatic criteria seems not to occur, a practice reinforced by the common belief that experiments cannot be conducted within the discipline because of the subject matter. In the materials sampled, no instrument was tested, and there was no effort to relate action based on economic theories to a particular outcome beyond some allusions to the effects of the 1961 tax cut. Finally, simple correlation or prediction is nowhere distinguished from an adequate causal relation—the two are collapsed. In economics, theories are sometimes tested for internal consistency, or for congruence with other economic theories with the same cognitive status, but such tests are very weak—a proposal for changing frogs into princes could easily survive such testing in the field of witchcraft. Economists rely almost entirely on predictive ability rather than on conjoining action and effect. Outside of econometrics, even references to predictive ability are actually rare. The doctrine of continuous testing, which is usually deemed an essential feature of the scientific enterprise, is nowhere to be found within economics or econometrics. Under the circumstances, the combination of approach to inquiry, procedures employed, and relation to data that characterize contemporary economics suggest that the policymaker regard all economic products as suspect pending adequate testing—inadequate until proven in action.

Unfortunately, the situation with respect to policymaking is unlikely to improve until a major reorganization of methodological fundamentals is carried out. Without a deliberate effort to determine the requirements for policymaking and to satisfy them with respect to economics, the common practice of collapsing prediction and control over events while ignoring the need for a causal assumption is likely to continue. The effect is to elasticize the meaning of theory, the very area in which adequate instruments are most badly needed, to a point where criteria of evaluation and improvement are impossible to enforce. Some insight into the extent of the confusion within economics is obtained from the exchange in the *American Economic Review (AER)* triggered by Paul Samuelson's comments on the problems of methodology.

Samuelson wrote first to attack Milton Friedman's assertion that the truth status of the premises in a model or theory did not matter so long as the model predicted accurately. The criticism was sound, and should have been decisive,but in passing Samuelson denied the methodological commonplace that a theory is wider or includes more information than any of its implications.[24] His aside drew a reply from Fritz Machlup, arguing (rightly, I believe) that accepting Samuelson's position would force economists to abandon *all* theories, and citing the appropriate references in philosophy of science. Moreover, Machlup called attention to the misconception of *theory* implied in Samuelson's assertion that deductions or predictions are made directly from theory, noting (again rightly) that predictions are made from a conjunction of theory and observation.[25] In a "Reply" published in the same issue of *AER,* Samuelson rejected the conception of *explanation* offered by Machlup.(In contemporary philosophy of science or methodology, to explain usually means to show that under specified limiting conditions application of an established theory to an observation effectively predicts the event to be explained.) The scientist, Samuelson said, could only "describe." An explanation, in Samuelson's view, was only a "more useful description that covers and illuminates a wider area."[26] However, to illustrate his meaning, Samuelson referred to a set of second-order differential equations used in a scientific theory, apparently not realizing that the point Machlup had raised was the disjunction between the singularity of a description, from which nothing can be inferred or deduced, and the generalized character of any instrument from which deductions or predictions could be derived.

Other voices were heard on the matter, mostly rejecting Samuelson's idiosyncratic view of the meaning of description, theory, and explanation. In due course, another "Reply" from Samuelson was heard. Although unrepentant and unreformed (a tribute to obstinacy if not perspicacity) he changed strategic positions by introducing a new concept—descriptions of "an empirical regularity" were now asserted to be the basis for scientific prediction.[27] Few economists honor David Hume, either in theory or practice, but few have disregarded his major contribution to the nature of observation and its limitations in so cavalier a fashion. By claiming that descriptions of generalized relations could be obtained directly from observation, Samuelson opened yet another methodological Pandora's box. But, the argument had by then run its course. By avoiding either a strict definition of description or a specification of the characteristics of the structures produced by the descriptive process, Samuelson was able to walk away from an extraordinary interchange unruffled. And that was a pity, for he was partly right and partly wrong and identifying each properly could have important consequences for the discipline. Both points had sufficient methodological and theoretical significance to warrant a fight to resolution. Unfortunately, academia has no arena for pursuing such mortal struggles to their final resolution and tradition opposes them in the name of "gentlemanly" conduct. Samuelson was right about the truth status of premises in theory or prediction and wrong about the concept of theory—the latter not because he differed from conventional views but because if his view is taken seriously it leads to anomalies and eventually a methodological dead end. In the confusion, Machlup's very important point about the need to combine theory with observation to generate predictions was lost. If voting with the pen is taken as a criterion, Friedman won the wrong argument for the wrong reasons; those who held that truth status of premises is irrelevant prevailed. The discipline lost on all counts.

   A different type of confusion, equally important in terms of its effect on economic products, arises from the postulational approach to theory that is common in the discipline. If theories are developed by postulation, from the top down rather than inductively, that suggests to observer or student that a valid theory will refer to a complex whole or entity—to an economic system, a subsystem such as banking or manufacturing, and so on. Economic theorists tend to look for an overarching structure roughly equivalent to the astronomer's treatment of the solar system, in contrast to the piecemeal development that has usually characterized science. The effects of this approach to theorizing are illustrated in a very striking way by a book review in the *Journal of Political Economy*.

An economic anthropologist named Frederick Pryor collected a number of assumptions or hypotheses relating to the economic aspects of primitive society, generated other assumptions himself, and tested the lot against a body of data obtained from a number of such societies. Disregarding the validity of the econometric procedures used, the reaction of the economist who wrote the review (Richard A. Posner) demonstrates the effects of theoretical holism better than any formal critique could. Pryor had written in his introduction: "The hypotheses studied in this book are not generated deductively from some overarching general model of primitive and peasant economies. Rather, I have combed the anthropological and economic literature for hypotheses of others and, in addition, have generated a large number by myself on the basis of simple economic considerations that scarcely warrant the rodomontade appellation of 'model.' " I find this view extremely sensible given the circumstances.

The reviewer's reaction speaks volumes about the effects of the holistic conception of theorizing:

How is one to characterize the hypotheses that are supported? . . . they are perhaps best described simply as a group of unrelated hypotheses that happen to pass Pryor's econometric tests. Indeed, Pryor announces at the outset of the book his lack of interest in theory. He presents himself to the reader as a pure empirical technician, whose self-assumed duty it is to test hypotheses by whomever proposed.[5] [Note #5 contains the citation to Pryor quoted above.]

There can be no quarrel with the division of labor; an individual's comparative advantage may lie in testing other people's hypotheses rather than proposing and testing his own. What makes Pryor's procedure curious, however, is the theoretical vacuum in which it occurs. It is not the case that there are well-developed rival theories of economic anthropology, one economic and the other anti-economic, one supported by his tests and one refuted by them. There is a rather formless anti-economic theory . . . which generates some testable hypotheses that Pryor tests. . . . But there is as yet no economic theory which generates the testable hypotheses that Pryor's econometric tests support. One cannot conclude that Pryor's work supports an economic approach to anthropology without first formulating an economic theory of primitive society and seeing whether it implies the hypotheses that he finds to be supported by the data.[28]

In the context of contemporary methodology, this is one of the more astonishing essays in print. The content may, of course, be a function of personal ignorance or idiosyncrasy. But the critique is entirely consistent with the approach to theorizing required by a postulational conception of theories, and since it entails at least four quite lethal assumptions (for theory and policymaking) about the nature of theory and the appropriate approach to inquiry, those errors are worth examining more closely.

First, the review clearly implies that theory must be developed *prior* to the creation of "low level hypotheses," and therefore prior to observation or the generalization of the results of observation. The theory must be created before its entailments are produced or tested. The inductive approach to theory is inverted; in the process, the value of developing and testing a simple relation between two observables is denied. Yet the history of science clearly suggests that establishing simple patterns of relations and subjecting them to continuous testing can be a fruitful point of departure for growth in any area with much human importance. Second, the reviewer assumes the possibility of a "theory of primitive society," an analog to a model of the solar system. But that is equivalent to asking for a "theory of physics" or "Why is a cow?" Physics is merely a label for a discipline and "Why is a cow?" is not a question. Theories refer to phenomena, usually changes, observed in the real world—the behavior of light, the effects of chemical action, and so on. They answer the question "why" but require a suitable object. Again, it is assumed there can be only one such theory, otherwise the relation between theory and hypothesis would not suffice to establish the "economic" character of the hypothesis. But for any genuine phenomenon, there can be any number of theories, an aspect of theorizing well known in economics. What makes a theory "economic" no one can say, for the usage is peculiar—no one speaks of a "physics theory" but of theories *in* physics. Similarly, the difference between theory and hypothesis is assumed but the basis for distinguishing the two is unspecified and in methodology is not common or important. Most important of all, the construction of theory allows deduction or prediction *from the theory alone* and not from a conjunction of theory and observation. That omission has the effect of transforming prediction into prophecy, for no reason could be offered to support it. In effect, the reviewer has borrowed his conception of science and theory, and his model of inquiry, from the Newtonian era, and more specifically from the astronomer's constructions of the solar system.

To this point, a policymaker determined to take the most favorable view possible with respect to the usefulness of the instruments produced within economics could argue that (a) some of those instruments are useful for making predictions and (b) the possibility of a causal relation among the variables, though not established, is not ruled out. However, three further aspects of economic inquiry remain to be examined: the kinds of assumptions incorporated into the instruments; the testing to which those instruments are exposed; and the normative adequacy of the structures. In combination with the critique already completed, they suffice to rule out using virtually all of the products of economics in reasoned policymaking.

THE QUALITY OF THE ASSUMPTIONS

In most of economics, the basic activity is model building, creation of formal patterns that can be used to predict events in the environment, or to explain them. Those models comprise sets of assumptions, premises, hypotheses, or relational statements; predictions are generated by calculating the implications of accepting those assumptions. A very large portion of the models and theories developed and used in economics, and not in economic theory alone by any means, contain premises or hypotheses that are palpably false, that do not correspond to experience. Many more incorporate assumptions whose truth status is uncertain, either because the information needed to test them is not available or because they cannot be operationalized and tested.

Much more than minor differences about secondary premises is involved. Some of the fundamental assumptions underlying major branches of economics are either known to be false or highly suspect. The "rational actor" assumption employed in large areas of economics, for example, is certainly false as an empirical proposition. The basic assumption in marginal analysis, that the businessman is a profit maximizer, could not be observably justified if only because the information required for testing it is not available.[29] The assumption in human capital theory that "an individual chooses the occupation and level of education that maximize the present value of his expected lifetime earnings'' is simply absurd, at least with respect to American society.[30] And the assumptions underlying welfare economics are even less credible, as Boulding points out,

It will no doubt be one of the great puzzles for future historians of thought as to how economists in the middle of the twentieth century managed to devise a whole discipline of welfare economics based on two absolutely preposterous assumptions. The first of these is the assumption of selfishness, that is, that the utility function of one person does not depend in any way on his perception of the welfare of another. The second even more preposterous assumption is that the preferences and the utility functions which express them are simply given, are not learned, and cannot be changed. The first assumption makes nonsense of the attempt of welfare economics to define a social optimum; the second makes nonsense of social and economic dynamics.[31]

At the level of the particular study, or the more limited model, the quality of the assumptions employed is no better. For example,

The model . . . describes an idealized monopolistically competitive system where all buyers are assumed to have identical preferences, and to possess full information on stores' offers. Demand is assumed to follow a uniform spatial distribution, and all stores are assumed to maximize profits under identical environmental conditions and resource endowments, and with perfect information.[32]

Or in another case,

It is assumed that firms have no a priori estimate of any single individual's skill vector. Instead, it is assumed that for the population as a whole, the probability distribution of the skill index is known with certainty. Further, the firm is viewed as drawing a random sample from the population.[33]

Such examples could be multiplied *ad infinitum.*

The reason for making such assumptions, obviously, is that they permit the solution of some specified problem—they allow formalization and calculation of the model for the situation. The effect, however, is to reduce models to toys. A model containing false premises is not only useless for policymaking, it cannot be used to make reliable predictions. The justification for that judgment is found in the internal structure of the instrument. If there is a logical system (S) that can be used to generate predictions, and one of its assumptions/premises/hypotheses is a rule in the form (A = 2B), then if that structure makes correct predictions about unobserved events in that form, changing the rule to A = B − 2 will certainly destroy its predictive value. Hence if the rule is "true" in one form, that is, corresponds to observation and experience, and "false" in another, there is no way to evade the conclusion that false assumptions must generate false predictions. That, as I understand it, was the point Paul Samuelson was trying to make against Milton Friedman in the controversy cited earlier in this chapter. Of course, it is always possible to create a predictive device by linking two wholly unrelated events according to rule—the number of fish caught in Alaska each month to the number of barrels of oil purchased from abroad in the succeeding month. To generate a prediction, the values of those two variables would have to be linked by rule; to generate a reliable and justifiable prediction, the rule would have to be true, that is, to express the relation actually observed in the past. If it were assumed that the two factors were related causally, that assumption is very likely to be false, and efforts to control the value of one by manipulating the other would not be justified. Confusing the two points, as seems to occur often in economics, has a devastating effect on the quality of the instruments produced.

Of course, a predicting device that incorporates rules of change that are known to be false can still be calculated; the logic is indifferent to the empirical meanings attached to the symbols. If that operation is carried out, it could turn out that some of the implications of the structure containing false assumptions actually fit real world observations. That is precisely what occurred with respect to Anthony Downs's *Economic Theory of Democracy,* cited above.[34] From a set of premises about rational behavior and its application to individual voting which were both false and known to be false by the author, a number of propositions was deduced and compared to events in real world elections. Some corresponded well; others did not. This was hailed as a genuine achievement, an example of what could be accomplished if "economic thinking" was transferred to politics. It was precisely that, of course, but not in the sense intended. The structure was cognitively inadequate when the predictions were made; there was no justification for accepting them *at that time,* a crucial point in testing procedure. Technically, the derivations were not predictions since structures incorporating false premises cannot predict in the meaningful sense of that term. The correspondence with observation of some derivations provided a basis for *post hoc* rationalization of the structure, but not a test. The instrument had, and has, no intellectual value or interest.

Within economics, the practice of including false assumptions in models or theories is frequently defended, usually by referring to Milton Friedman's essay on methodology.[35] A careful reading of the essay shows that Friedman evaded and obfuscated on the issue and in no way resolved it. Indeed, his reasoning is very curious given the content of the rest of the essay. For Friedman identifed a theory as a "hypothesis that yields valid and meaningful predictions about phenomena not yet observed," and argued that "the only relevant test of the *validity* of a hypothesis is comparison of its predictions with experience." His main point with reference to the quality of the assumptions in a theory is that it is wrong to suppose "that hypotheses have not only 'implications' but also 'assumptions' and that the conformity of these 'assumptions' to reality is a test of the validity of the hypothesis *different from* or *additional to* the test by implications." There can be no argument on that point. Friedman then proceeds to a needlessly complex examination of the possible role that "assumptions" can play in theory. In the process, he certainly conveys some highly misleading impressions, most notably in the following passage:

> In so far as a theory can be said to have 'assumptions' at all, and in so far as their 'realism' can be judged independently of the validity of predictions, the relation between the significance of a theory and the 'realism' of its 'assumptions' is almost the opposite of that suggested by the view under criticism. Truly important and significant hypotheses will be found to have 'assumptions' that are wildly inaccurate descriptive representations of reality, and, in general, the more significant the theory, the more unrealistic the assumptions (in this sense).[36]

Now, I must confess that I am unable to determine from the essay precisely what an assumption is in the sense intended, let alone to identify a meaning that was both tenable and would allow the statement quoted to hold. To cut through the verbiage, however, it is only necessary to point out that the statement of relations contained in a theory, and every theory consists of one or more such statements, is in Friedman's sense a "hypothesis," and can therefore be tested against "the conformity of its implications or predictions with observable phenomena." In that context, to say that an assumption is false is to claim that some statement of relations does not conform to observation—precisely the point that Boulding made about the assumptions in welfare economics. Friedman could hardly disagree. And using Friedman's test, many of the fundamental assumptions on which economic theory depends are false and not merely inexact. The instruments that depend upon them are therefore useless for dealing with real world affairs.

TESTING

The competent policymaker searching economics for useful instruments will find few that claim to incorporate the causal relation needed, but a substantial number of models for which predictive capacity is asserted. The weight of evidence clearly supports the judgment that useful tools are not likely to be found among them, but an adequate and sustained testing program could, presumably, identify those able to perform the needed functions. Again, however, the policymaker is stymied, for the models and theories produced by economists remain largely untested, even for purely predictive uses, as are the underlying assumptions of the models, which are crucial for determining their usefulness in policymaking. As Tjalling Koopmans told the American Economic Association in 1978, "We do need to find ways in which verification of the premises of economics through cumulative econometric analysis and through experiments that find a sponsor can be pursued." Subsequent remarks made it clear that little progress was being made. "I have not found in the literature a persuasive account of how such confirmation of premises can be perceived and documented."[37] Testing, or development of supporting evidence, has not been one of economics' strong suits.

From a slightly different perspective, economics is not an experimental discipline in the customary sense of that term. There is no evidence of the continuous interplay of theory and observation that is usually regarded as the ultimate guarantor of scientific knowl-

edge. Tests need not be performed in a laboratory to provide justification for theory; indeed, natural state testing is far more con-
vincing than laboratory evidence, other things equal. The primary
consideration is development of a cyclic pattern of exchanges between the real world and the theorists seeking to deal with it. The
kind of purely formal "tests" or "experiments" sometimes cited
by economists are quite meaningless, however illustrious the economist involved: ". . . we perform an experiment. . . . In the first
case, we raise $p_1$, the price . . . while holding constant the quantity
of the second input . . . the rise in $p_1$ must lower $v_1$ as shown by the
negative slope of the light curve through A."[38] Regardless of the
meaning attached to the various symbols in the example, all that is
tested by such procedures is the logical consequences of changing
some dimension of a formal model.

The most common form of testing within economics, and more
particularly in econometrics, uses predictive accuracy as the basic
criterion—a base that is *at best* extremely weak from the policymaking perspective. Consider the following set of conclusions to a
paper dealing with the effectiveness of fiscal policy.

There is a strong theoretical justification from micro-economics for the
proposition that even anticipated government actions affect real variables.
On a macro-economic level, this proposition has received some support
in my work in the sense that a number of "micro-economic" explanatory
variables are significant in my estimated equations.

. . . the equation that I have estimated to explain Fed behavior . . . appears
to be good when judged by conventional statistical standards.

A method that I have proposed for estimating the expected predictive
accuracy of economic models indicates that my model is more accurate
than Sargent's model, Sim's model or a naive model, with respect to forecasts of real GNP, the GNP deflator, and the unemployment rate.[39]

Even if all of the conclusions are conceded in full, nothing useful
for policymaking can be found in the structure.

The internal evidence available in published economics rules out
the assumption that the instruments deployed there have been tested
adequately for policymaking in all but a few cases. There are too
few citations of data, too little evidence obtained from observation
of the effects of action, too few signs of deliberate experimentation,

whether in the laboratory or in society at large. I have yet to see an economic theory that incorporates a statement of limiting conditions for use, which is a little like manufacturing an automobile without wheels. References to the reliability of theories do not appear. Such phrases as "We tried X . . ." or "We did X . . ." are not found in the published materials of the discipline. None of the institutional arrangements that would be needed to test and monitor effectively are in place—not even a decent inventory of initial state conditions, nor have there been strong demands from economists to generate such baseline data. One expects the skunk to have scent glands and a creature without them is regarded with suspicion when it is claimed as a member of the species. The absence of the paraphernalia for testing and experimenting carries a strong message, or warning, for the policymaker.

The long-range implications of current practices with respect to testing and justification of theories or models in economics are perhaps even more disquieting than the short-run effects on policymaking. Indeed, the capacity to deal with economic problems effectively may have to be developed within government for lack of accomplishment within the academic establishment. For economists seem increasingly to be immune to data requirements and unconcerned with the need for testing and justification by evidence. In combination with the practice of developing theory by postulation rather than inductive procedures, such immunity could seriously impede development of the kind of knowledge that reasoned policy demands. Most economic theorists seem not to believe that the results of observation should be consulted before and during the theorizing process; the evidence suggests there is little compulsion within individual or discipline to take theories to the real world for testing; and in some cases, the results of testing are simply ignored. In effect, the absence of evidence, the inability to test, or even counterevidence, seems not to matter. Here, for example, the problem is simply brushed aside: "No attempt has been made in this study to quantify or test for the existence of such preferences. Indeed, the results of any such attempt would likely be of limited value."[40] Occasionally, the position is stated more bluntly and directly, though the result is intellectually no more satisfactory, as in this statement: "Testing implications of the theory are difficult to derive, and testing itself presents serious problems. Defense of the approach [Public Choice] comes down, quite simply, to the faith that 'some theory is better than nothing.' ''[41] If the concept of theory is sound, that judgment is acceptable. Given the quality of economic inquiry, the position is untenable; there are no *prima facie* reasons for assuming that any medicine is an improvement over no medicine, or that resorting to patent medicine is better than knowing that no treatment is available.

The tendency for economic theorists to evade testing by creating theories that are beyond test, or theories that are too difficult to apply is annoying, and leads one to wonder what purposes such activities serve. The capacity of such theories and approaches to survive in the face of overwhelming evidence of inapplicability of even evidence of error is disturbing and not merely annoying. The mathematical theory of games, and formal information theory, for example, have defied best efforts to apply them to social problems—there is almost no possibility of satisfying their minimum conditions for application—yet inquiries that depend on them continue almost unabated. And approaches or theories have not only refused to bow to the contrary evidence; they have refused steadfastly to do so much as nod. A particularly good example is found in the application of "public choice" economics to legislative decisionmaking. As a recent article pointed out: "Theoretical work by several authors suggests that a minimum winning coalition (MWC) will determine the decisions of a legislature making distributive policy." (Here follow citations to the work of William Riker, Buchanan and Tullock, Riker and Ordeshook, and others.) "These scholars conclude that the majority will adopt distributive policies that benefit themselves at the expense of the minority. These authors also predict that majorities will be of the barest possible size, since MWC maximizes the per capita gains for the winners," however, "empirical studies of Congress uniformly find that the [MWC] prediction is simply wrong. Nearly all studies report that members of legislatures seek unanimity and are reluctant to exclude minorities from the benefits of redistributive legislation."[42] The theoretical structure in question is derived from "rational actor" assumptions. The original statement of the theory was published in 1962; a restatement in 1973 virtually ignored empirical criticism—indeed, the act of publication is reasonably construed as a refusal to face facts.[43]

An even more ominous practice, so far as the integrity of inquiry is concerned, is the development of a device for rationalizing theory that allows the theorist to ignore either theoretical or empirical challenges. It depends on the assumption that what is important is the logical consistency of the set of assumptions employed in theorizing. It apparently originated within "public choice" economics but could presumably be applied to any area of inquiry, as shown in the following passages:

Any covering law or laws used as a rationalization of existing empirical conditions may be challenged by alternative propositions that can equally well predict similar conclusions. Public choice analysis does not respond to such theoretical challenge to its rationalizations by crucial hypothesis testing. . . . Nor need it be content with an apparent inconsistency between alternative covering laws. . . . Instead, it searches for new theoretical concepts that can form higher level propositions that can, in turn, rationalize its covering law or laws. Such higher level propositions can "explain away" the apparent inconsistency. . . . The evidence interpreted in this form of analysis is judged by the logical consistency of its propositions. . . .

The requirement of logical consistency among its theoretical propositions allows the theoretician to interpret the empirical evidence as confirmatory or to explain away apparently disconfirmatory evidence by developing higher level propositions. Grounding public choice analysis in such logical empiricism therefore offers security to the paradigm and renders it impregnable to assaults of rival theories.[44]

The case is extreme, of course, but it stands as a reminder of the weakness of the constitutional safeguards available against intellectual dogmatism or tyranny—the antidote, methodological competence, is in very short supply.

Finally, in the same vein, the extent to which economists can differ dogmatically on economic matters, and accuse one another of ignoring the evidence or serving as hired gun to particular interests, is somewhat disturbing to an observer who is uncertain whether it is a family quarrel marked by the usual exaggerations or a case of *in vino veritas* with the heat of argument substituting for the heat engendered by wine. What is to be made of John K. Galbraith's appeal to Milton Friedman to make an honest assessment of the evidence being generated within Great Britain of the effects of monetarist policies?

Friedman has shown himself over the years to be both an able and an agile protagonist. If inflation and idle plant and unemployment persist in Britain in the face of his policies, he will be tempted to wiggle, and he does this with commanding skill. Control of the money supply was not wholly in accordance with his requirements . . . another year was necessary for a true test. . . . I would urge Prof. Friedman to resist such excuses.[45]

Now, the attack can simply be dismissed as another instance of politics in economics, and that may indeed be the case. But the *Guardian,* perhaps for reasons of its own, printed an accompanying note which quoted Friedman's call for "more time" in the British experiment, coupled with a strong attack on those who were administering the program, "The civil service and the Bank of England have been unbelievably incompetent. I am almost inclined to use stronger terms." What can the critic say in the circumstances?

NORMATIVE INADEQUACY

The empirical contribution to policymaking must suffice for two basic purposes: first, to project the set of alternatives from which choice must be made, to determine the prospective costs and benefits of action; second, to generate a strategy for achieving the preferred alternative. The statement of costs and benefits will be made, obviously, in terms of the normative variables employed by the policymaker, whether that is a society or an individual. The adequacy of any theoretical contribution to policymaking is assessed at least partly in terms of the completeness of the costs and benefits that are projected. Putting the requirements this way calls attention to a point too easily overlooked in empirical inquiry: as the purpose of agriculture is to supply food, to feed people, so the purpose of economic activity is to provide the goods and services that people want and need. The significance of economic activity lies outside economics, as with any other empirical discipline. To the extent that economics seeks to contribute to human ability to control economic activity, it becomes willy-nilly dependent upon the normative structure for guidance—which may be one reason why conservatives prefer to leave such matters to "natural" processes and rely on prediction alone as the purpose of inquiry. If the conception of inquiry cuts economics off from the noneconomic effects of economic activity, it serves to define away human problems. And since it then cannot generate an adequate statement of the costs and benefits of the available options it cannot be used by the policymaker.

It is obvious from what has already been said about economics that in normative terms it is utterly inadequate for policymaking. That inadequacy tends to be overlooked within the discipline on the mistaken assumption that empirical inquiry is in no way concerned with normative affairs. That may be true for a pure science, if such a discipline is possible, but no field of study that purports to be useful for making policy can adopt that position. Far more is involved here than radical complaints against conservative bias, however important that may be in certain contexts—comparison of one economic system with others, for example. The inadequacy is readily demonstrated: costs and benefits must ultimately be displayed in terms of the effects of action on suitably aggregated populations and neither the conceptual apparatus or the theoretical structures required for that purpose are currently available within economics. Moreover, there is not so much as awareness of need, in most cases, let alone any serious effort to fill it. And it should be said, in all fairness, that the conceptual apparatus needed for the task is not available in moral philosophy either, and will in due course have to be created.

The principal sources of inadequacy are easy to locate but difficult to remedy. They lie in the focus of inquiry on the "economic system," and the assumption that empirical and normative inquiries are wholly separate enterprises. Given these conditions the conceptual apparatus cannot include the normative terms needed to display benefits and costs. The theoretical apparatus ceases to function at the boundaries of the economic system yet the normative implications of economic activity are external to the economic system. Any effect that cannot be captured in the network of concepts developed for exploring the structures and processes of the economic system will be lost. So long as economics maintains that limit, it cannot in principle fulfill the policymaker's requirements.

The dilemma has been recognized within economics, implicitly at least, and two procedures have been used for dealing with it. The first is to take a uniconceptual or "cost-free" approach to social problems, concentrating on a single phenomenon to be controlled and ignoring side effects. The common expression for initiating the approach is for the economist to say to the policymaker, "Tell me the goal you are trying to achieve and I will tell you how to achieve it.'' That may sound reasonable, but it avoids two essential steps in the process. First, policymakers cannot select a goal until they know the options; second, the costs and benefits of the options must be stated as fully as knowledge permits. For example, an economist, pressed for an example of the usefulness of economic knowledge, selects the task of reducing the flow of automobile traffic into New York City, and recommends the imposition of a tax, of unspecified amount, on each automobile entering the city. Raising the tax, the economist contends, will reduce automobile flow to any desired level. In one limited sense, that is a "solution" to the traffic problem, but it is a solution with no cost-benefit analysis attached and it cannot be used. The policymaker must know what else will happen, for serious rioting or economic stagnation might be too high a price to pay for the desired reduction in traffic levels. The conceptual and theoretical apparatus is simply inadequate. The analog is the physician who promises to remove a wart from the finger but amputates the whole arm—the treatment succeeds, but the physician is unlikely to have many repeat customers.

The other device used to avoid the normative problem has been the development of internal criteria for evaluating the state of the economic system, as a whole or in part. Explicit in welfare economics, the general procedure is implicit in most of the subfields as well. In principle, no solution to the normative problem can be produced in that way; the separation of economics from the rest of human life guarantees against it. But economists have been remarkably successful in gaining acceptance for such evaluative criteria. Utility maximization, which is utterly meaningless in real world affairs, has become an accepted criterion for dealing with individual and collective choices. Such system states as "competitive equilibrium," "Pareto optimality," "full employment with stable prices," or a particular rate of growth with price stability all belong to the same class of evaluative terms. Assuming they could be operationalized, which is doubtful, they would remain empty for they refer to system states and the things valued lie outside system boundaries—the economic system is not valued intrinsically. The emptiness is reflected in their meaning: maximization ignores the dimensions of things maximized; competitive equilibrium ignores the welfare implications of income distribution; Pareto optimality does not take into account the initial distribution of resources within society;

and full employment, as Joan Robinson rather angrily insisted, means nothing until the ends it serves are identified.

It is worth recalling at this point that the criteria used are a function of the initial assumptions on which the approach to inquiry depends. Economists are not moral monsters who care nothing for people just because their recommendations may have very unfortunate consequences for large populations—though they may be judged moral monsters for other reasons. Economic advice depends on the conception held of the economist's task, the capacity available, and the strategy lines open to the actor. That is one reason for insisting so strongly that improvement of economics must begin at the base, with the fundamental approach to inquiry or the purposes sought in inquiry. When economists chide one another for normative inadequacy, they simply demonstrate the absence of a shared conception of the discipline. The present consensus tends to place the economist in a position somewhat analogous to the physician who is unconcerned with the effects of his treatment on patients.

Economics parallels a political science stripped of such concepts as oppression, tyranny, invidious distinctions, or justice. Parallel conditions are found *within* the economic system yet they elude the economist's conceptual apparatus. For example, there is a well-known tendency for competition in a price-oriented society to degrade the product to the lowest possible level. Yet there is apparently no room in economic theory for assessing the performance of the system in these terms, or even identifying unwanted side effects. The tasteless berries, flabby chickens, and other food products whose nutritive qualities and even health effects have been modified radically in the thrust for profit maximization (or increased production) would seem to be a serious dimension of economic activity. Yet information about such matters must usually be supplied from outside economics, and economics supplies no remedies.

At another level of normative inadequacy, economists in the United States have failed to provide the information needed for judging among competing alternative economic systems, or even adjustment of the current economic system in terms of its consequences. In general, the consuming public (of economic systems) has been provided with dogma rather than data, even through the educational system. System malfunctions tend to be ignored or suppressed; positive achievements are overstated and overpublicized, often in a grossly invidious manner. It is improper, for example, to compare standards of living in two countries with different economic systems; the proper comparison lies between the conditions to be expected in any one country under two different systems. In that restricted sense, economics has pandered to the established system in the manner of Voltaire's Dr. Pangloss. Yet for the whole society, choosing an economic system is perhaps the most important choice to be made, and that includes the choice of modifications in present practices. In that choice, society is surely entitled to some assistance from economics.

## A NOTE ON ECONOMETRICS

On the surface at least, econometrics seems a more likely source of assistance with reasoned policymaking than economic theory or general economics.[46] The heart of the econometric enterprise is construction and fitting of formal models to real world data, what Herman Wold has called experimental and nonexperimental model building. That seems a much more promising approach to useful instruments than the postulational methods commonly used in economic theorizing. But the usefulness of the enterprise depends on the performance characteristics of the models, on the assumptions built into them and the criteria of adequacy applied to them. Here, the differences between economic theorizing and econometrics are much smaller than might be supposed. The latter has great potential, but it has not been exploited effectively. Some of the work carried out in econometrics closely resembles experimental science, but it is only a tiny fraction of the whole. The bulk of econometrics remains fairly close to ordinary economic theorizing, accepting the same purposes, and pursuing them by much the same means. Moreover, there has been a decided tendency for econometricians to devote very significant amounts of time and energy to purely technical questions, procedures for manipulating data or various kinds of statistical tests, for example. Without an adequate conception of the purposes of inquiry, the requirements for reasoned policymaking, the normative factors involved, and the kinds of tests and evidence that should be employed, econometricians are no more likely to satisfy the requirements for policymaking than are economic theorists. At the global level, the policymaker is as unlikely to find useful instruments within econometrics as within economic theory.

That judgment refers mainly to what may be called "campus econometrics" in the United States, the works published in standard academic sources. The quality of product available within the business community may be much better. Econometric studies produced within government may also be of higher quality, though it should be noted that the studies published by agencies of the national government, or by such "captive" bodies as the Urban Institute or the Brookings Institution are unimpressive. Indeed, they tend to support Galbraith's assertion that economic projections and prescriptions published by governments are statements of hopes, aspirations, and needs and therefore should not be taken seriously.[47] Whether the results achieved by such agencies as the national planning bodies in Western Europe (the Netherlands, for example) are significantly better than the products of American academia is not known but is unlikely. The potential of present-day econometrics, given free rein and full access to information, is almost impossible to assess. But there are fairly good reasons to believe its capacity is very limited, particularly with respect to the needs of policymaking.

The reasons for assuming limited capacity are compelling. Econometrics is part of economics, and employs much of the conceptual-theoretical apparatus developed there. It therefore shares many of the same weaknesses, although there is considerable variation among practitioners. Econometrics has not developed a strong commitment to supplying the needs of policymakers, and there has been no systematic effort to determine the character of those needs and how they might be fulfilled.[48] The traditional commitment to "science" rather than engineering remains strong and if the rhetoric of policy relevance is common, it has not been supported by actions aimed at producing the needed institutional arrangements and criteria of adequacy. Most econometricians are as uncertain about the goals of inquiry as are the economic theorists. Pragmatic criteria are nowhere employed to test the models produced. In most cases, the stated purpose of the econometrician remains the same as the purpose of the theorist, to develop a formal structure that can predict and explain, using the latter term in the ordinary statistical sense.

The conceptual apparatus, with all of its limitations, has been borrowed intact from economics. The approach is holistic, with the economic system serving as the central focus for inquiries and the Newtonian approach to the solar system serving as a paradigm for inquiry. The new terms that appear in econometrics refer to the techniques of analysis rather than the substance of economic experience. Indeed, most of the models produced within econometrics depend on the theories developed within general economics. Both the empirical and the normative inadequacies found in economic theory reappear in econometrics unchanged. Although econometricians make use of what are called "policy variables" in their analysis, they do not refer to the consequences of action for specific populations, nor do they measure costs and benefits in human terms. Most of the purposes and practices are simply transferred from general economics. Econometrics shows no sign of having developed out of a commitment to purpose outside traditional economics; rather it appears as a different way of achieving more or less traditional purposes.

One reason why the products of econometrics are rarely useful in policymaking is the astonishing portion of total publications devoted to technique and method. Doubtless *Econometrica* serves as the primary vehicle for disseminating information about new techniques and procedures, and could therefore be expected to contain more technical and procedural matter than might otherwise be the case. But 90 to 95 percent of the major articles published in the 1970s dealt with such procedural questions or techniques; very few indeed contained applications of those techniques or somehow demonstrated their usefulness. The policymaker working through the major journals could discard nine of ten articles after a prefunctory inspection of the contents. Indeed, the reader is at times lead to wonder how the discipline was established with so little technical capacity, or, if the capacity was available why it has not been used effectively and the results published. Econometricians spend a great deal of time creating and grinding axes and very little time cutting timber.

For the policymaker, the prime weakness in econometrics, as in economic theory, is the failure to establish, or to look for, a causal relation among the variables included in the model. Deliberate efforts to establish a causal relation are rare. As noted earlier, the need to incorporate a causal assumption in econometric models intended for use in policymaking has long been recognized, particularly in the line of development that began with Jan Tinbergen. But the criteria for testing causality developed by C.W.J. Granger at the end of the 1960s remained the best procedural base available in the early 1980s. Granger's test is clear and easy to apply: if data series X is better predicted by a universe that includes series Y than by a universe in which it is not included, then series Y is a cause of X.[49] Unfortunately, prediction alone is no more conclusive with respect to causality than the application of John Stuart Mill's "methods," which serve as the philosophic base for all such techniques. Moreover, if there are interactions among the variables (inaccurately expressed in the term feedback) then a four-element set is in practice beyond calculation and a five-element system cannot be calculated in principle. Not one of the articles in econometrics sampled contained an adequate justification for assuming a causal relation—and *every* article published during the 1970s that dealt with substantive problems was examined. Only rarely was a causal relation so much as mentioned. In most cases, the author focused on predictive capacity and ignored the causal relation. On that count alone, virtually all of the products of econometrics are *prima facie* inadequate for policymaking.

Further, it should be said that econometrics shows as few signs of becoming an experimental enterprise as does economic theorizing, and for much the same reasons. Without reference to use or some pragmatic criteria, there is no base for improvement beyond predictive accuracy and that is inadequate. Although the situation may be different in government or business, academic econometrics is characteristically a one-shot affair that is very unlikely to lead to improvements in the instruments produced. As in theory, it would be extremely difficult to create the kind of close relations with government or business that would provide needed real world problems, the genuine constraints that adequate policymaking must respect, and the opportunities for applying and monitoring effects that are needed for improvements over time. What is particularly disturbing here is the absence of claims to performance. When events have been successfully managed by the use of theories, the theorists concerned are unlikely to sit quietly in the wings. The 1961 Kennedy tax cut was regarded as a demonstration of the validity of monetary and fiscal policy for years; although the grounds were extremely dubious it is cited endlessly by those who favor such actions. Examples of problems successfully managed using econometric methods, econometric models, or even econometricians cannot be found. Where there is no smoke, the observer is inclined to suspect there is no fire either.

Two other areas of potential weakness in econometrics deserves to be noted, though they cannot be treated adequately in a short note. First, the question whether or not a particular econometric technique has been applied properly, and whether the cognitive status of the result is adequate for policymaking given the data available and the techniques employed, should be examined in every proposed application of the results of econometrics—at least until the discipline is more firmly established.[50] The point is not that technique may be abused, for that occurs everywhere. But in fundamental methodological terms, the underlying approach to inquiry is unlikely to be any more sophisticated in econometrics than in general economics and that lack of sophistication and awareness will be reflected first in the misuse of technique. The inadequacy of econometric tests of causality, which depends ultimately on some reference to the effects of use or application, illustrates the point. Exploration of the limits and uses entailed by the purely formal and technical dimensions of econometrics is sorely needed if the modest survey carried out here is even approximately typical. The task lies well beyond my competence in statistics or knowledge of econometrics, but those concerned with policymaking need a stringent examination of the real world implications of the various statistical conventions and techniques currently used in analysis. A partial and tentative examination of some current practices leaves the nonexpert sorely troubled at lacunae and apparent inadequacies in the inferential structure.

The second weakness, well known to econometricians themselves, is that quality of the data employed in econometric models is poor and problematic. Any body of information can be viewed as stored experience, and that gives it potential value. But actual worth is a function of current purpose, the theoretical requirements of fulfilling that purpose, and the way in which the data were collected and stored. When data have been aggregated improperly, or created for a different purpose, they may not be adequate. Information collected and made available by the national government (Bureau of the Census, Internal Revenue Service, or Bureau of Labor Statistics, for example) vary enormously in quality and usefulness. Census figures, for example, have been widely used for dealing with all sorts of social and economic problems. But with respect to major elements of the population, and particularly those residing in the larger cities, accuracy is very questionable. To illustrate, a comparison of the number of persons living in a five-digit zip

code area in the city of St. Louis in 1970 with the number of payment recipients living there as recorded by the Social Security Administration suggested an undercount of as much as 200 percent. Further,
measured turnover rates in some areas were over 50 percent in a
single year. Similar criticisms are appropriate with respect to other
statistics such as unemployment figures published by the Bureau of
Labor Statistics, for the counting methods exclude many who are
genuinely unemployed but have either not been employed previously,
or have been unemployed too long. The undercount of unemployed
black youth is perhaps best known but similar errors occur with
other populations. No one knows the actual level of unemployment
within the population. In fact, there is no sound basis for estimating
the adequacy of the estimates.

Such considerations are not new, of course, but the fact that
econometrics does not usually produce its own data, and has relatively little influence over their quality, suggests a substantial discount
on certain kinds of policy recommendations. That is particularly
important where variables used in analysis have been synthesized,
that is, indexed in some fashion. The dangers are often noted,
though the practice continues, and is indeed hard to avoid. The
results can be utterly worthless, witness the following critique:

Here we have a case in which synthetic data can give essentially nonsense
results, and yet if the nonsense accords with our beliefs . . . there is little
incentive to question the validity of the procedure followed in obtaining
the results.

. . . if there is such potential for nonsense where data are openly constructed, what hidden links exist in data constructed and named by others
that are thrown indiscriminately into statistical analysis?. . . we would urge
maintaining an awareness of how variables have been constructed, even
after they have been given a name or symbol for expository or notational
convenience.[51]

To which can only be added, amen!

The practice of using aggregated data in econometrics poses
some exceptional problems for the policymaker, even if the requirement for radical individualism in choices is relaxed. Obviously, any
kind of event can be aggregated and generalized, and the methods
of econometrics find good uses in fields such as medicine where the
unit of analysis in choice or action is clearly the individual. Much
depends on methods of aggregation, for policy must be made at

the point where data can no longer be disaggregated—and that need not be the individual. Aggregates are then treated by a common policy, assumed to be affected in the same manner by a common action, whatever the heterogeneity of the aggregate at the level of action. The issue is most easily probed by asking whether a "saturation" policy is acceptable given what is known of an aggregate and the techniques used to produce it. That is, if the effects of action are relatively homogeneous across wide populations, costs are low, and side effects are minimal, such saturation techniques as mass vaccination are an easy way to produce a desired outcome such as immunity from a particular disease. But as mass influenza vaccinations demonstrated in recent years, if costs and side effects are significant, the mode of aggregation should rule out the use of such techniques on reasoned grounds. Alternatives are impossible to produce for populations that are heterogeneous with respect to several important characteristics.

The last illustration of the problems encountered when a holistically oriented discipline uses aggregated data to develop theory can be found in the various foreign economic assistance programs funded by the federal government. For decades, it was assumed without question that increasing national income or the gross national product would over time produce improvements in the conditions of life of nearly everyone in the society. Indeed, the assumption that the effects of aggregate change will somehow "trickle down" to the lower economic strata of society continues to be accepted in domestic affairs. But the evidence available in foreign assistance clearly contradicts the assumption. In some parts of Latin America, increases in national income have in fact been accompanied by a significant decrease in the living conditions of the poorer segments of the population. Those driven from marginal subsistence farming into urban poverty by the change to cash crop agriculture, for example, are clearly worse off than before.[52] The antidote to such errors is to examine the effects of policy on individuals and not to rely on changes in features of society as criteria of success. The solution is more easily stated than achieved.

## NOTES

1. William S. Reece, "Charitable Contributions: New Evidence on Household Behavior," *American Economic Review* 69 (March 1979): 149-50 (hereafter cited as *AER*).

2. Ibid., p. 22; p. 38; p. 71; pp. 84, 94. It is interesting to note that all of these illustrations come from a single volume of *AER*.

3. *AER* 67 (September 1977): 557.

4. *AER* 64 (May 1974): 319.

5. Cited in Robert A. Gordon, "Rigor and Relevance in a Changing Institutional Setting," *AER* 66 (March 1976): 1-14.

6. *Journal of Political Economy* 88 (June 1980): 460.

7. *AER* 62, no. 3 (June 1972): 368; *AER* 62, no. 4 (September 1972): 640.

8. George J. Stigler, *The Citizen and the State: Essays on Regulation* (University of Chicago Press, 1975), p. 53.

9. For examples, see "The Crisis in Economic Theory," *The Public Interest*, Special Issue (1980); David Mermelstein, "The Threatening Economy," *New York Times Magazine*, December 30, 1979, or articles by R. J. Ball and T. Burns, D. Laidler, and M. H. Miller in *AER* 66 (September 1976).

10. Kenneth E. Boulding, *Collected Papers*, ed. Fred R. Glahe (Colorado Associated University Press, 1971), vol. 1, pp. 127-28.

11. The quotation is taken from Wassily Leontief, *The Economic System in an Age of Discontinuity* (New York University Press, 1976); printed in Wassily Leontief, *Essays in Economics: Theories, Facts and Policies*, vol. 2 (Basil Blackwell, 1977), p. 153.

12. Herman A. Wold, "Econometrics as Pioneering in Nonexperimental Model Building," *Econometrica* 37 (July 1969): 369-81.

13. See pp. 165-66.

14. Milton Friedman, "The Methodology of Positive Economics," in his *Essays in Positive Economics* (University of Chicago Press, 1953), p. 7; James M. Buchanan, "Economics and Its Scientific Neighbors," in *The Structure of Economic Science: Essays on Methodology*, ed. Sherman R. Krupp (Prentice-Hall, 1966), p. 182.

15. Emile Grunberg, "The Meaning of Scope and External Boundaries of Economics," in Krupp, *Structure of Economic Science*, p. 149.

16. Friedrich A. von Hayek, *Full Employment at Any Price?* Occasional Paper 45 (London Institute for Economic Affairs, 1975), p. 42.

17. Gordon, "Rigor and Relevance," p. 3.

18. See Robert E. Butts and John W. Davis, eds., *The Methodological Heritage of Newton* (University of Toronto Press, 1970), especially an essay by Norwood R. Hanson. See also John Hicks, *Causality in Economics* (Basil Blackwell, 1979), pp. 31-32.

19. Richard B. McKenzie and Gordon Tullock, *The New World of Economics: Explorations into the Human Experience* (Richard D. Irwin, 1975), ch. 1.

20. Anthony Downs, *An Economic Theory of Democracy* (Harper and Brothers, 1957), p. 6.

21. Ibid., p. 8.

22. Wassily Leontief, "Theoretical Assumptions and Nonobserved Facts," *AER* 61 (March 1971): 25.

23. James M. Buchanan, "Public Goods and Public Bads" (Mimeograph of paper delivered at the 1970 meeting of the Public Choice Society, Chicago, Ill., n.d.), pp. 4-5. ". . . self-interested behavior of individuals in a competitive market produces socially-desired results."

24. Paul A. Samuelson, "Problems of Methodology—Discussion," *AER* 53 (May 1963): 231-36.

25. Fritz Machlup, "Professor Samuelson on Theory and Realism," *AER* 54 (September 1964): 732-35.

26. Ibid., pp. 736-39.

27. "Professor Samuelson on Theory and Realism: A Reply," in *The Collected Scientific Papers of Paul A. Samuelson,* ed. H. Nagatani (MIT Press, 1966), vol. 3, pp. 765-73.

28. Frederick Pryor, introduction, *The Origins of the Economy* (Academic Press, 1977); book review by Richard A. Posner in *Journal of Political Economy* 88 (June 1980): 606-11.

29. Kenneth E. Boulding, *Economics as a Science* (McGraw-Hill, 1970), p. 67.

30. David A. Wise, "Academic Achievement and Job Performance," *AER* 67 (June 1975): 351.

31. Kenneth E. Boulding, "The Network of Interdependence" (Mimeograph of paper delivered at the 1970 meeting of the Public Choice Society, Chicago, Ill., n.d.), p. 1.

32. Pinhas Zusman, "Welfare Implications and Evaluation of Buyer's Travel Inputs and Nonprice Offer Variations in Networks of Retail Stores," *Econometrica* 37 (July 1969): 440.

33. Kenneth I. Wolpin, "Education and Screening," *AER* 67 (December 1977): 951.

34. See note 20, above.

35. Friedman, "Methodology of Positive Economics."

36. Ibid., p. 14.

37. Tjalling C. Koopmans, "Economics Among the Sciences," *AER* 69 (March 1979): 11-12.

38. Paul A. Samuelson, *Collected Scientific Papers,* vol. 3, p. 9.

39. Walter Dolde, "Temporary Taxes as Macro-Economic Stabilizers," *AER* 69 (May 1979): 90.

40. Cotton M. Lindsay, "Medical Care and the Economics of Sharing," in *Theory of Public Choice: Political Applications of Economics,* eds. James M. Buchanan and Robert D. Tollison (University of Michigan Press, 1972), p. 60.

41. James M. Buchanan, in ibid., p. 122.

42. Barry R. Weingast, "A Rational Choice Perspective on Congres-

sional Norms," *American Journal of Political Science* (May 1979): 245.

43. William H. Riker, *The Theory of Political Coalitions* (Yale University Press, 1962) contained the original statement; compare William H. Riker and Peter C. Ordeshook, *An Introduction to Positive Political Theory* (Prentice-Hall, 1973).

44. Mark Sproule-Jones, "Public Choice and Natural Resources: A Methodological Explication and Critique," mimeographed (1980).

45. John K. Galbraith, "Running Out of Excuses," *Washington Post,* reprinted in *Guardian,* October 26, 1980, p. 15.

46. For the scope of econometrics, see *Econometrica* 39 (July 1971). It contains a brief report on the Second World Congress of Econometrics, held in Cambridge, England, together with a summary of other meetings, which indicate the primary concerns of the discipline at the beginning of the decade sampled.

47. John K. Galbraith and Nicole Salinger, *Almost Everyone's Guide to Economics* (Houghton Mifflin, 1978), pp. 8-9.

48. Yet the discipline has been criticized for being too closely linked to policymaking, see T. W. Hutchison, *Knowledge and Ignorance in Economics* (University of Chicago Press, 1977).

49. See C.W.J. Granger, "Investigating Causal Relations by Econometric Models and Cross-Spectral Methods," *Econometrica* 37 (July 1969): 424-38 and R. Ashley, C.W.J. Granger, and R. Schmalensee, "Examining Causality by Econometric Methods," *Econometrica* 48 (July 1980): 1149-67. Additionally, N. Georgescu-Roegen, "Methods in Economic Science," *Journal of Economic Issues* (June 1979); A. Zellner, "Causality and Econometrics," *Journal of Monetary Economics* (Supplement, 1979): 9-54, includes commentary by C. A. Sims and C. R. Nelson. See also a review of Hubert M. Blalock, Jr.'s *Causal Inferences in Nonexperimental Research* (University of North Carolina Press, 1964) by Herman A. Wold in *Econometrica* 33 (October 1965): 879-80.

50. For an example, see Harvey S. Rosen and Kenneth T. Rosen, "Federal Taxes and Homeownership: Evidence from Time Series," *Journal of Political Economy* 88 (February 1980): 59-75. The problem dealt with is a counter-to-fact-conditional (If A had been different than B would be different), a proposition that requires a very rigorous theory for satisfactory justification. There is no evidence whatever of awareness of that dimension of the problem, or the uselessness of statistical techniques in that situation. See Nelson Goodman, *Fact, Fiction, and Forecast* (Bobbs-Merrill, 1965) for the logical requirements.

51. John A. Carlson and James R. Frew, "Money Demand Responsiveness to the Rate of Money Return on Money," *Journal of Political Economy* 88 (June 1980): 606.

52. See Eugene J. Meehan and Charles A. Reilly, "Local Level Develop-

ment in Rural Latin America: The IAF Experience," in *Progress in Rural Extension and Community Development,* eds. Gwyn E. Jones and Maurice Rolls (John Wiley, 1982); William C. Thiesenhusen, "Reaching the Rural Poor: A Goal Unmet," in *International Perspectives on Rural Sociology,* ed. Howard Newby (John Wiley, 1978); Cheryl A. Lassen, *Landlessness and Rural Poverty in Latin America,* Monograph no. 4 (Cornell University, 1979).

_____6_____ 

# Pessimistic Postscript

Examined systematically in terms of the instrumental requirements for reasoned policymaking, the highly regarded capacity of contemporary American economics is only an illusion. Individual publications, regardless of length, rarely if ever supply the tools that policymakers must have. Since the overall approach to inquiry and theorizing exemplified in publications is woefully inadequate, improvement in the near future is extremely unlikely. Granted that the substance of academic publications may not reflect the discipline's capacity to deal with real world affairs, the underlying methodological-epistemological assumptions, revealed in the particular case, effectively rule out adequate real world performance in precisely the same way that inadequate piano technique, revealed in playing particular pieces, rules out high quality performance in concert. More specifically, the approach to inquiry, the conception of theory, the relation to observation and data, the kinds of instruments sought, the assumptions employed in economic models, the testing procedures used, and the normative basis of performance must all be rated inadequate with reference to policymaking. Unless changes are made in each of these areas, future improvements in performance cannot be expected.

What is perhaps surprising is the relative absence of criticism from consumers of economic knowledge. Occasionally, someone involved in policymaking will break silence and complain, but the overall impact of economics on society's policymaking performance remains largely uncriticized. To some extent, that situation can be attributed to the spirit of optimism with which complaints are usually terminated. In 1970, when Sherman Maisel of the Federal Reserve Board pointed out, with surprising candor, that little was known of the relation between Board actions and real world consequences, it created quite a stir. The *New York Times* reporter noted with some amazement that "if all of the 15 or so men who have most to say about the government's economic policy were agreed on what the target for the economy next year should be, they would not be at all sure how to hit it." But there was no demand for either explanation or action. The "openness" of the speech was applauded, and it was conjectured that "economists may be learning this lesson faster than others," for open market operations were ". . . now being done with more humility."[1] The choice of words is interesting, for nearly ten years later, George W. Ball concluded an acid critique of the policy advice supplied by economists on the same note: "Humility is, however, the first requisite to understanding, and it is comforting to discover economists who are at least privately admitting that they no longer have full confidence in their own omniscience."[2] Neither judgment corresponds very well to the impression conveyed by economic publications at the time, or by subsequent developments in the discipline.

The reference to humility, to the need for awareness of the limitations inherent in the economic enterprise, is apt if not accurate. For if economics is to be useful in policymaking, providing such assistance must become the primary objective of inquiry. Identifying and pursuing the instruments that policymakers must have cannot guarantee success but without that commitment it can almost be guaranteed to fail. The faults in the structure of assumptions on which economics proceeds are too numerous to be remedied by accident or through piecemeal improvements. A deliberate and systematic effort to learn what is required is essential. I have tried to suggest some of the major areas in which changes will have to be made, and show why they are necessary.

The tragic dimension of the illusion is the double bind in which the consumer is trapped. First, an economics that is inadequate for making policy nevertheless impacts countless millions of lives, in much the same way that patent medicine impacts the health of its users. Second, the prestige and influence that economics presently commands within academia and in the community at large effectively deters improvements in the discipline unless a major change occurs in public and private attitudes and support—a change that is very unlikely in the short run. Perhaps the most unfortunate side effect of the situation is the apparent willingness of society to continue to accept and apply system-state criteria of the performance of the economy and not to insist on a clear reckoning of the costs and benefits of individual and collective action, rendered in human terms. Since those criteria control allocation of the bulk of society's collective resources, the full effects of the illusion are immense if incalculable.

In similar fashion, the prestige of economics facilitates the continued export of the "economic" approach to inquiry into the other social sciences. An effort to commit American political science to the study of a political system closely analogous to the economic system but derived from systems analysis dominated the field for most of the 1950s.[3] Since then, the inflow from economics has been steady, and unfortunate. The "collective choice" or "public choice" approach to inquiry has flourished since the 1960s, though accomplishments have fallen far short of claims.[4] A "social indicator" movement, also grounded in economics, has sought ways of inventorying social conditions that could be used in policymaking and evaluation for nearly two decades. Despite large expenditures, the enterprise has foundered on inadequate initial conceptualization, yet it has succeeded in monopolizing the effort, and continues to do so at the time of writing.[5] Even public administration has been a periodic target for invaders from economics[6] There is, of course, nothing wrong in principle with borrowing from other fields. But in this case, the lethal inadequacies in the field of economics have been included in the exported commodity. Accomplishments have been minimal, particularly with respect to policymaking, but the activities flourish.

Considering the history of the recent past and the present state of the discipline, there seems little possibility of a major change within economics that would improve performance for policymaking.

Pressure would almost certainly have to be exerted from outside the discipline. The only genuine possibility seems to be the development of competitive capacity within government, or in some kinds of special institutions, and neither is likely. For one thing, competent consumership of economic products would be required, along with a set of social institutions able to make use of the knowledge. Development and staffing of such capacity *outside* of economics is a social impossibility for all practical purposes. A genuinely experimenting society requires an adequate economics, as well as other social sciences; barring a disaster so massive that the whole society would have to be rebuilt, such disciplines are unlikely to appear in the short run. As they operate at present, governments very often do not want sound information and decent theories, or even accurate statements of the costs and benefits of the available options. In that context, cynicism suggests that an economics without real capacity may be perfectly suited to assist and advise a government that neither desires nor intends doing anything not established in historic practice.

Within the discipline, system inertia remains dominant, despite occasional protests from youth. Control over the channels of expression and influence is firmly vested in the elderly. To improve the training provided budding economists, major changes would be needed in the criteria used to locate faculty, in the evidence accepted for retention and promotion, in the standards of publication applied by journals and presses, in the distribution of support from public and private foundations, and in the overall relations between government and university. Such changes are unlikely to the point of absurdity.

What is particularly discouraging is the kinds of criticism voiced within economics. The intellectual grounds on which economics could build a fruitful approach to inquiry have not appeared. The self-criticism presently indulged by economists, though often sharp and pointed, will not produce the needed changes even if it succeeds, for it is misdirected. The primary reason for pessimism on this score is the relative absence of adequate methodological or epistemological criticism within the discipline, for that is where primary adjustments must be made. The apparent unwillingness of economists to take such criticisms seriously when they do appear does not bode well. The fundamentals remain untouched.

Some concrete evidence of the importance of the underlying assumptions is provided by the development of the *Journal of Post-*

*Keynesian Economics* (JPKE), established in 1978. The initial statement of purpose was relatively unexceptionable:

The need for a general scholarly journal receptive to innovative theoretical work that can shed fresh light on contemporary economic problems has become imperative. The *Journal of Post-Keynesian Economics* is conceived as such a publication. Its aim is to encourage evolving analysis and empirical study to contest the conformist orthodoxy that now suffuses economic journals in the United States. [It] . . . will be committed to the principle that the cumulative development of economic theory is possible only when the theory is continuously subject to challenge, in terms of its ability to explain the real world and to provide a reliable guide to public policy.[7]

The aim is laudable and the reasoning sound. But materials published in *JPKE* were little better than those in the *American Economic Review* so far as usefulness in policymaking is concerned. Good intentions without capacity are not enough. Either the critical apparatus were not available or the kind of material required did not appear. Although early issues of JPKE challenged orthodoxy, they did not set forth an adequate alternative to established economic practices or suggest an approach to inquiry likely to produce improvements. The challenge remained at the level of the disciplinary subdivision; the underlying structure of assumptions remained intact.

The inadequacy of economic self-criticism is particularly apparent in the use made of one major channel available for criticizing the discipline, the major address to the annual meeting of the American Economic Association (AEA). That platform, from which a very large number of economists can be reached, was used occasionally during the decade to express dissatisfaction with the discipline's performance. More often, criticism was avoided, and even in those cases where the speaker was critical, the quality and content of the criticism remained inadequate if the goal is improved performance in policymaking. The three strongest critics heard in the 1970s were Wassily Leontief, Joan Robinson, and R. A. Gordon.[8] Their criticisms were directed at the tendency to formalism within economics, the willingness to sacrifice relevance for logical rigor, and the inadequacy of the theoretical apparatus. Theory in particular was singled out for very sharp comment, as in Robinson: "I am talking about the evident bankruptcy of economic theory, which, for the second time, has nothing to say on questions that, to everyone

except economists, appear to be most in need of an answer."[9] But
the grounds for the complaints were poorly articulated. There were
few concrete proposals for improvement; none attacked the intellectual foundations of the discipline. And the critics themselves
provided no examples of the kinds of improvements that could be
made. It is one thing to assert that economists have nothing to say
and another matter to demonstrate that nothing can be said given
the mode of inquiry followed in economics. Complaints were not
couched in the form of diagnosis and prescribed treatment supported by clinical evidence. Significantly, none of the critics suggested the need for a pragmatic criterion of performance.

Further, major addresses to the national convention of economists
are not uniformly, or even usually, critical of economics. Most
commonly, the validity or usefulness of the discipline is simply taken
for granted and the opportunity is used to carry out a conventional
economic exercise.[10] Occasionally, the speaker heaps praise on the
intellectual achievements of the discipline, or even claims to apply
economics successfully:

The applicable principles are easy to characterize: that economic efficiency
calls for prices equated to marginal social opportunity costs, and that
whenever it is technologically feasible, competition is the best institutional
mechanism for achieving that result as well as minimizing X-inefficiency
and ensuring the optimum rate of innovation.[11]

These claims are typically vacuous, for such principles are impossible to apply, however readily they may be characterized. But the
sense of self-satisfaction conveyed by the paper is representative.

The most interesting form of self-criticism in economics comes
from the conservative right. There, a pronounced tendency to defend economics while denouncing economists is the rule. Milton
Friedman's defense of monetary policy at the 1971 AEA meeting is
a good example.

My final conclusion is . . . that monetary policy did not fail in the past
three years in the relevant scientific sense. The drug produced the effect
to be expected, though the wrong drug was administered and the patient
expected it to be far more potent than it was capable of being.[12]

Friedman faulted economists for disseminating false views of
economic capacity. Economic theory is defended; the suppressed
assumption is that economists both now and in future, can do

no better, that nature must dispose and man must learn to live with the disposition. The point is strongly urged in the peroration:

We have been driven into a widespread system of arbitrary and tyrannical control over our economic life, not because "economic laws are not working the way they used to," not because the classical medicine cannot, if properly applied, halt inflation, but because the public at large has been led to expect standards of performance that as economists we do not know how to achieve.[13]

Friedman's line of reasoning was carried to its logical extreme by Friedrich Hayek in a Nobel Lecture that must have left the members of the selection committee squirming in their seats. Decrying efforts to imitate physical science or to apply scientific standards to economics, Hayek flatly rejected positive efforts to control the human destiny by human actions and denounced the fatal striving to "control society rather than leave the natural forces to work themselves out."[14] The same animus can be discerned in recent efforts to limit the governments freedom of action in economics by constitutional restrictions on the total money supply, or to reestablish the gold standard.[15] This type of criticism classifies economic activity with such natural forces as earthquakes and tides; human reason may capture the form and predict the event but control lies beyond human competence. Economics is construed fundamentally as a spectator sport.

Those who take a position similar to Hayek or Friedman could, of course, be correct. The recent history of economics provides little basis for optimism. Nevertheless, the position cannot be defended *in principle,* whatever the empirical evidence. The reasons for the present inadequacy of economics *can* be identified, and there is no reason in principle why they could not be circumvented. I consider such changes unlikely, particularly in the short run. But they are not impossible. And that is perhaps all we are entitled to ask.

## NOTES

1. Edwin L. Dale, Jr., "Imprecise Tools Used in Money Policies," *New York Times,* December 6, 1970.
2. George W. Ball, "An Overdose of Economists," *Washington Post,* April 20, 1980.
3. David Easton, *The Political System* (Alfred A. Knopf, 1959); idem, *A Systems Analysis of Political Life* (John Wiley, 1965).

4. Thomas R. deGregori, "Caveat Emptor: A Critique of the Emerging Paradigm of Public Choice," *Administration and Society* (August 1974): 205-28 is critical. For a friendly overview, see Dennis C. Mueller, *Public Choice* (Cambridge University Press, 1979). The rationalist position is best stated in James M. Buchanan, and Gordon Tullock, *The Calculus of Consent* (University of Michigan Press, 1962).

5. For criticism, see Eugene J. Meehan, "The Social Indicator Movement," *Frontiers of Economics: 1975* (University Publications, Blacksburg, Va., 1976), pp. 27-43; idem, "Social Indicators and Policy Analysis," in Frank P. Scioli, Jr., and Thomas J. Cook, *Methodologies for Analyzing Public Policies* (Lexington Books, 1975), pp. 33-46.

6. For examples, see Norman Frohlich and Joe A. Oppenheimer, *Modern Political Economy* (Prentice-Hall, 1978); William A. Niskanen, Jr., *Bureaucracy and Representative Government* (Aldine, 1971); or Hans van den Doel, *Democracy and Welfare Economics,* trans. Brigid Biggins (Cambridge University Press, 1979).

7. *Journal of Post-Keynesian Economics* 1, no. 1 (1978): 1-7.

8. Wassily Leontief, "Theoretical Assumptions and Nonobserved Facts," *AER* 61 (May 1971): 25; Joan Robinson, "The Second Crisis of Economic Theory," *AER* 62 (May 1972): 9-10; Robert A. Gordon, "Rigor and Relevance in a Changing Institutional Setting," AER 66 (March 1976): 1-14.

9. Robinson, "Second Crisis of Economic Theory."

10. Robert M. Solow, "The Economics of Resources and the Resources of Economics," *AER* 64 (May 1974): 1-14.

11. Alfred E. Kahn, "Applications of Economics to An Imperfect World," *AER* 69 (May 1979): 17.

12. Milton Friedman, "Have Monetary Policies Failed?" *AER* 69 (May 1979): 17.

13. Ibid.

14. Friedrich A. von Hayek, *Full Employment at Any Price?* Occasional Paper 45 (Institute for Economic Affairs, London, 1975): 32-42.

15. For example, "one solution, only, is practically available, namely that of enshrining the control of inflation in the form of a monetary constitution, which eliminates governmental control over the money supply in favor of nondiscretionary expansion of rates that reflect the underlying rate of real growth of the economy in question. Such a constitution by reducing the scope of Leviathan, in fact would protect citizens from short term political manoeuvres in a finite election period, and, in a fundamental sense, would safeguard the democratic order," Charles K. Rowley, and Alan T. Peacock, *Welfare Economics: A Liberal Restatement* (Martin Robertson, 1975), p. 190.

# Selected Bibliography

Andrain, Charles F. *Politics and Economic Policy in Western Democracies.* Duxbury Press, 1980.

Arrow, Kenneth J. *Social Choice and Individual Values.* 2d ed. (Yale University Press, 1963).

———. *Essays in the Theory of Risk-Bearing.* Markham, 1971.

Ascher, William. *Forecasting: An Appraisal for Policy-makers and Planners.* Johns Hopkins Press, 1978.

Ashby, W. Ross. *An Introduction to Cybernetics.* Science Editions, 1963.

Bauer, Raymond A., ed. *Social Indicators.* MIT Press, 1966.

Berlinski, David. *On Systems Analysis.* MIT Press, 1976.

Bish, Robert L. *The Public Economy of Metropolitan Areas.* Markham, 1971.

Blalock, Hubert M., Jr. *Causal Inference in Nonexperimental Research.* University of North Carolina Press, 1964.

Boulding, Kenneth E. *Collected Papers.* Edited by Fred R. Glahe. 5 vols. Colorado Associated University Press, 1971-1975.

———. *Economics as a Science.* McGraw-Hill, 1970.

Braithwaite, Richard B. *Scientific Explanation: A Study of the Function of Theory, Probability, and Law in Science.* Harper and Brothers, 1960.

Buchanan, James M., and Tollison, Robert D., eds. *Theory of Public Choice: Political Applications of Economics.* University of Michigan Press, 1972.

Buchanan, James M., and Tullock, Gordon. *The Calculus of Consent: Logical Foundations of Constitutional Democracy.* University of Michigan Press, 1962.

Campbell, Norman. *What is Science?* Dover Publications, 1952.

Davidson, Paul. *Money and the Real World.* 2d ed. Macmillan, 1978.

Downs, Anthony. *An Economic Theory of Democracy.* Harper and Brothers, 1957.

Dror, Yehezkel. *Public Policymaking Reexamined.* Chandler, 1968.

Dubin, Robert. *Theory Building.* Rev. ed. Free Press, 1978.

Fishburn, Peter C. *The Theory of Social Change.* Princeton University Press, 1973.

Flax, Michael J. *A Study in Comparative Urban Indicators.* Urban Institute, 1972.

Fox, Karl A. *Social Indicators and Social Theory.* John Wiley, 1974.

Friedman, Milton. *Essays in Positive Economics.* University of Chicago Press, 1953.

————. *Capitalism and Freedom.* University of Chicago Press, 1963.

Frohlich, Norman, and Oppenheimer, Joe A. *Modern Political Economy.* Prentice-Hall, 1978.

Galbraith, John K., and Salinger, Nicole. *Almost Everyone's Guide to Economics.* Houghton Mifflin, 1978.

Goodman, Nelson. *Fact, Fiction, and Forecast.* Bobbs-Merrill, 1965.

Hardin, Garrett. *The Limits of Altruism.* Indiana University Press, 1977.

Hayek, Friedrich A. von. *The Counterrevolution of Science.* Free Press, 1952.

Hempel, Carl G. *Aspects of Scientific Explanation and other Essays in the Philosophy of Science.* Free Press, 1965.

————. *Philosophy of Natural Science.* Prentice-Hall, 1966.

Hicks, John. *Causality in Economics.* Basil Blackwell, 1979.

Hollis, Martin, and Nell, E. J. *Rational Economic Man.* Cambridge University Press, 1975.

Hutchison, T. W. *Knowledge and Ignorance in Economics.* University of Chicago Press, 1977.

Klein, Lawrence R. *The Keynesian Revolution.* Macmillan, 1961.

Krupp, Sherman R., ed. *The Structure of Economic Science: Essays in Methodology.* Prentice-Hall, 1966.

Kyberg, Henry E., Jr., and Nagel, Ernest, eds. *Induction: Some Current Issues.* Wesleyan University Press, 1963.

Lakatos, Imre, and Musgrave, Alan, eds. *Criticism and Growth of Knowledge.* Cambridge University Press, 1970.

Leontief, Wassily. *Essays in Economics.* 2 vols. M. E. Sharp, 1976 and 1978.

————. *Structure, System, and Economic Policy: Proceedings of Section F of the British Association for the Advancement of Science.* Cambridge University Press, 1977.

Lowe, Adolph. *On Economic Knowledge: Toward a Science of Political Economics.* Harper and Row, 1965.

Machlup, Fritz. *Methodology of Economics and Other Social Sciences.* Academic Press, 1978.

McKenna, Christopher K. *Quantitative Methods for Public Decision Making.* McGraw-Hill, 1980.

McKenzie, Richard B., and Tullock, Gordon. *The New World of Economics: Explorations into the Human Experience.* Richard D. Irwin, 1975.

Malinvaud, E. *Statistical Methods of Econometrics.* North Holland Publishing Co., 1970.

Meehan, Eugene J. *The Quality of Federal Policymaking: Programmed Disaster in Public Housing.* University of Missouri Press, 1979.

————. *Reasoned Argument in Social Science: Linking Research to Policy.* Greenwood Press, 1981.

Mishan, E. J. *Welfare Economics: An Assessment.* North Holland Publishing Co., 1969.

————. *Economics for Social Decisions: Elements of Cost-Benefit Analysis.* Praeger, 1972.

Morris, Morris D. *Measuring the Conditions of the World's Poor: A Physical Quality of Life Index.* Pergamon Press, 1979.

Mueller, Dennis C. *Public Choice.* Cambridge University Press, 1979.

Nagel, Ernest. *The Structure of Science: Problems in the Logic of Scientific Explanation.* Harcourt, Brace and World, 1961.

Nagel, Ernest, and Newman, James R. *Godel's Proof.* New York University Press, 1958.

Niskanen, William A., Jr. *Bureaucracy and Representative Government.* Aldine, 1971.

Okun, Arthur M. *Equality and Efficiency.* Brookings Institution, 1974.

Okun, Arthur M., and Perry, George L., eds. *Curing Chronic Inflation.* Brookings Institution, 1978.

Olson, Mancur. *The Logic of Collective Action: Public Goods and the Theory of Groups.* Harvard University Press, 1965.

Peacock, Alan T. *The Economic Analysis of Government and Related Themes.* Martin Robertson, 1979.

Popper, Karl R. *The Logic of Scientific Discovery.* Science Editions, 1961.

————. *Objective Knowledge: An Evolutionary Approach.* Oxford University Press, 1972.

Quine, Willard V. *Word and Object.* MIT Press, 1960.

Revlin, Russell, and Mayer, Richard E. *Human Reasoning.* V. H. Winston, 1978.

Rieke, D., and Sillars, Malcolm O. *Argumentation and the Decision-Making Process.* John Wiley, 1975.

Routh, Guy. *The Origins of Economic Ideas.* Macmillan, 1975.

Rowley, Charles K., and Peacock, Alan T. *Welfare Economics: A Liberal Restatement.* Martin Robertson, 1975.

Samuels, Warren J., ed. *The Methodology of Economic Thought.* Transaction Books, 1980.

Samuelson, Paul A. *The Collected Scientific Papers of Paul A. Samuelson.* 4 vols. MIT Press, 1966-1977. Vol. 1 edited by Joseph E. Stiglitz, vol. 2 edited by R. C. Merton, vol. 3 edited by H. Nagatani, vol. 4 edited by K. Crowley.

Schelling, Thomas C. *Micromotives and Macrobehavior.* W. W. Norton, 1978.

Simon, Herbert A. *Models of Man.* John Wiley, 1957.

Smyth, R. L., ed. *Essays in Economic Method.* McGraw-Hill, 1962.

Stigler, George J. *The Citizen and the State: Essays on Regulation.* University of Chicago Press, 1975.

Suppes, Patrick. *The Structure of Scientific Theories.* 2d ed. University of Illinois Press, 1977.

Tinbergen, Jan. *Shaping the World Economy.* Twentieth Century Fund, 1962.

―――. *International Economic Integration.* 2d rev. ed. Elsevier, 1965.

―――. *Economic Policy: Principles and Design.* North Holland Publishing Co., 1967.

Toulmin, Stephen. *The Philosophy of Science: An Introduction.* Harper and Row, 1960.

Tullock, Gordon. *Private Wants, Public Means: An Economic Analysis of the Desirable Scope of Government.* Basic Books, 1970.

van den Doel, Hans. *Democracy and Welfare Economics.* Trans. Brigid Biggins. Cambridge University Press, 1979.

Weintraub, Sidney. *Capitalism's Inflation and Unemployment Crisis: Beyond Monetarism and Keynesianism.* Addison Wesley, 1978.

Weintraub, Sidney, and Davidson, Paul. *Keynes, Keynesians, and Monetarists.* University of Pennsylvania Press, 1978.

# Name
## Index

# Subject
## Index

## About the Author

EUGENE J. MEEHAN, who received his Ph.D. from the London School of Economics, is Professor of Political Science and Staff Urban Planner at the University of Missouri-St. Louis. He is the author of several books including *Reasoned Argument in Social Science* (Greenwood Press, 1981), *Foundations of Political Analysis,* and *Programmed Disaster in Public Housing.*